Advanced Excel
Interview Questions
You'll Most Likely Be Asked

Job Interview Questions Series

www.vibrantpublishers.com

Advanced Excel Interview Questions
You'll Most Likely Be Asked

© 2012, By Vibrant Publishers, USA. All rights reserved. No part of this publication may be reproduced or distributed in any form or by any means, or stored in a database or retrieval system, without the prior permission of the publisher.

ISBN-10: 1475188358
ISBN-13: 9781475188356

Library of Congress Control Number: 2012906686

This publication is designed to provide accurate and authoritative information in regard to the subject matter covered. The author has made every effort in the preparation of this book to ensure the accuracy of the information. However, information in this book is sold without warranty either expressed or implied. The Author or the Publisher will not be liable for any damages caused or alleged to be caused either directly or indirectly by this book.

Vibrant Publishers books are available at special quantity discount for sales promotions, or for use in corporate training programs. For more information please write to **bulkorders@vibrantpublishers.com**

Please email feedback / corrections (technical, grammatical or spelling) to **spellerrors@vibrantpublishers.com**

To access the complete catalogue of Vibrant Publishers, visit
www.vibrantpublishers.com

Table of Contents

1.	General Questions	7
2.	Formulae	41
3.	Problems	65
4.	VBA / Coding	75
5.	Specific Uses	89
6.	Graphs, Drawing and Pictures	101
7.	HR Questions	119
	INDEX	133

This page is intentionally left blank

Advanced Excel Interview Questions

Review these typical interview questions and think about how you would answer them. Read the answers listed; you will find best possible answers along with strategies and suggestions.

This page is intentionally left blank

General Questions

This is to test a range of questions relating to the software itself rather than to its use.

Installation

1: If you have bought one copy of Microsoft Excel 2010 and have installed it on your computer, under what conditions are you allowed to install it on a second machine?

Answer:
Obviously you could de-install it from one and put it on a second. But the question is about installing on a second at the same time as the first. The answer being sought is that you can install another copy of the software on a portable device for use by the single primary user of the licensed device.

Notes: This is in the Microsoft Software license terms, Section 2b (accessible from File -> Help). It may seem like small print, but it can save someone a lot of money.

Leap Years

2: In real life, leap years are divisible by 4 but not by 100 unless they are also divisible by 400. So we get:

1800	Not leap year
1900	Not leap year
2000	Leap Year
2100	Not leap year
2200	Not leap year
2300	Not leap year
2400	Leap Year
2500	Not leap year

What does Excel do with these years (i.e. is there a 29th February in these years in Excel)?

Answer:
This is harder than it looks because there are two parts to the answer and both must be identified for the answer to be correct. Firstly, dates in Excel start at 1st January 1900. Thus it does not treat days before 1900 as dates and thus 1800 cannot be stored as a date in Excel. Secondly, there is a well-documented bug in Excel (which have been there over many versions) as it treats the year 1900 as a leap year. Thus it will happily store the 29th February 1900 even though the

date never existed and it will claim there are 2 days difference between 28th February 1900 and 1st March 1900.
Notes: The first is critical if you are planning to use Excel to store historical dates (such as the dates of the kings of England). The second catches people out from time to time and can delay a project for a considerable amount of time as the error can be very difficult to track down.

Worksheets
3: What is the shortcut key to insert a new worksheet into the workbook?
Answer
Shift-F11
Notes: Quick keypress, especially useful if you will want a lot of worksheets.

Cursor keys stop working
4: I have been working on my spreadsheet for some time and now suddenly when I press the down arrow, the current cell does not move down one cell, but the whole spreadsheet moves up one cell on the screen. So my cursor, which was originally on cell B5 is still on cell B5. What has happened and how do I fix it?
Answer:
You have pressed the Scroll-lock key. Press it again to go back to "normal" mode.
Notes: Can be a useful mode if you are showing the spreadsheet to someone.

Current time and date
5: You want to put the current time into cell B4 and the current date into cell C4 (as static text, so that they won't change as time passes). What is the quickest way of doing this?
Answer:
 a) In cell B4, press Control and : (colon) and then press Enter.
 b) In cell B4, press Control and ; (semi-colon) and then press Enter.
Notes: Often used when recording activities (e.g. it happened on Ctrl-; date at Ctrl-:)Not a formula question as it is just a keyboard

operation.

What's going on?
6: In the following picture, what is the user doing?

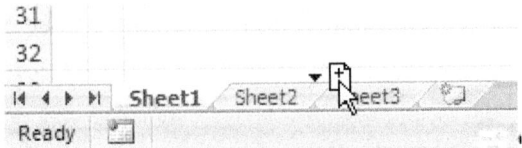

Answer:
The user is copying the worksheet "sheet1" by holding down the control key.
Notes: The user is not moving the worksheet, or there wouldn't be a plus in the image of the sheet.

Shop locations
7: You have a list of locations for your fifty shops. You will often need the list put into spreadsheets. What method can you use to speedily put them in when you need them? Where would you find this functionality?
Answer:
Clearly you could start writing code, but there is a much easier way. Add the list of your shops as a custom fill series. Then, whenever you want them just type in the first one and drag down.
The functionality is under File -> Options -> Advanced and then Edit Custom Lists, as shown:

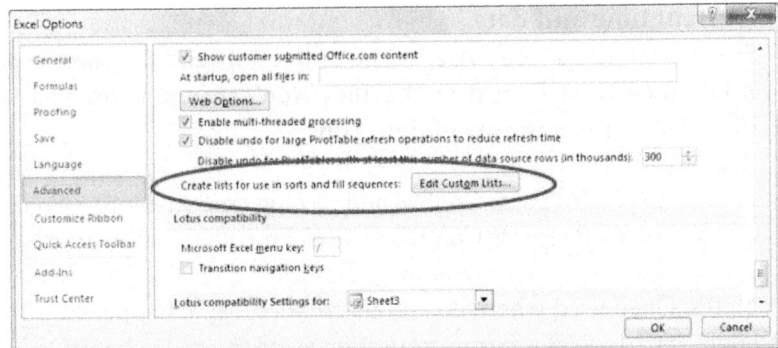

Notes: It's a very nice procedure because it doesn't require writing any code and can be used at any time.

Coloring gridlines
8: Obviously you could use borders to change the colors of any of the edges of the cells, but (without using borders), how do you change the colors of all the gridlines?
Answer:
If you go to File -> Options -> Advanced, there is an option for you to select what color your gridlines could be.

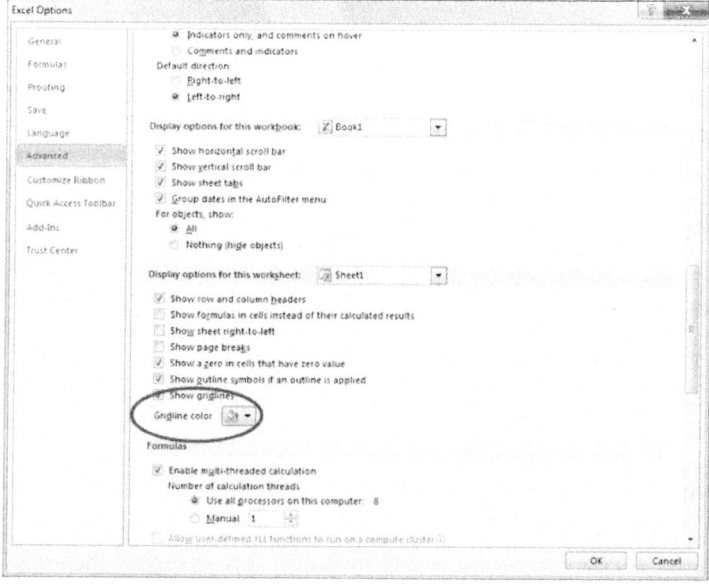

Iterative calculations
9: When would you enable iterative calculations?
Answer:
When you (intentionally) have circular references and want Excel to go round the circle a limited number of times.
Notes: Usually circular references are entered erroneously, but there are times when the circle gets you closer and closer to the best solution, and you want to run the circle a number of times to get a close enough approximation of the optimal solution.

Taking control
10: What happens if, after typing the following formula into cell A8, you press Control + Enter, instead of just Enter?
=sum(a1:a6)
Answer:
The formula is entered normally, but the current cell does not move on.
Notes: This is designed to make people who don't know the right answer guess a wrong one. For example, the content of the formula is not relevant to the answer nor is the fact that you are summing A1 to A6 and missing A7 when you put the formula into A8.

Moving round a large sheet
11: You have a large spreadsheet - many rows and columns. What are these keyboard shortcuts for?
  a) Going down by a page of data
  b) Going up by a page of data
  c) Going right by a page of data
  d) Going left by a page of data

Answer
  a) Page Down
  b) Page Up
  c) Alt + Page Down
  d) Alt + Page Up

Notes: Clearly answers a) and b) are obvious. However it was easier to ask for all four than to try and explain that we only wanted left and right. As people get more advanced on spreadsheets, they tend to use keyboard shortcuts more and the mouse less. Thus the shortcuts that are really wanted but less used are important.

Show Page breaks
12: When you set your print area, it is the trigger for Excel to show you the Page Breaks. How do you put an icon onto the Quick Access Toolbar to turn these Page Breaks on and off?
Answer:
There is no direct way, so you have to create a macro to turn them on or off and then create an icon to invoke the macro.
Notes: Most functions can be added directly to the Quick Access

Toolbar. This is an example of one that is not available.

Drop down lists
13: Without using form controls, how do you create a drop-down list in a cell?
Answer
   a) Create the list in a set of cells
   b) On the cell(s) you want the list to appear, use Data Validation (in the Data ribbon)
   c) In the Settings tab, there is an "Allow" dropdown. Pick "List" from it. (see picture below)
   d) Select the list of cells to validate
   e) Click OK

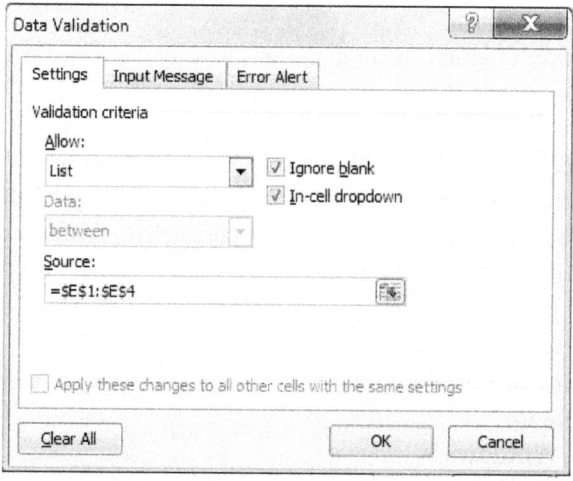

Notes: You can also do something similar with form controls. However form controls float on top of the spreadsheet, not fitting into the cells.

Currency
14: You have the number 125 in the current cell (which is quite wide). What happens when you click the highlighted button on the home page?

Answer:
The currency symbol will appear on the left of the cell, the number will have ".00" put after it, and the number will otherwise be right-aligned.
Notes: Note that the currency symbol ($) will be separated from the number. This is so that the numbers are easier to read.

Going round in circles
15: What is a circular reference?
Answer:
Any formula which either includes itself, or does so indirectly, for example in cell C1 there is the formula:
=sum(A1:E1)
As the cell C1 is in the range, it is a circular reference.
Notes: Most of the time circular references are an error. It is possible for a circular reference to be legitimate, but you would need to limit the number of calculations or Excel would be calculating forever!

Platforms
16: Which of the following platforms is a version of Microsoft Excel available for?
- a) Windows
- b) Mac OS X
- c) Linux
- d) BSD
- e) Unix

Answer:
a) Windows and b) Mac OS X only
Notes: Between 1989 and 1991, there was a version of Excel for OS/2 as well, but this was not asked about as it has not been around since then.

What's the difference?

17: What is the difference between a database and a spreadsheet?
Answer:
At first thought this seems obvious. After all, databases are made up of tables with rows and columns of data. And then you think that so are spreadsheets.

Basically there are various differences, but the most fundamental one is that databases have an inherent structure between the tables whereas spreadsheets do not. Look for words like "relational".

Notes: There are factors such as spreadsheets are generally single user, smaller, number based, used for ad-hoc calculations, and so on. These are differences, but a database can also do these (though it may not be the best tool for the job).

Adding data
18: You have a large spreadsheet (many rows and columns) and are in the middle of it when you need to enter a new line. What is the quickest way of getting to the start of the next empty row at the bottom of the spreadsheet?
Answer:
Press Shift-F4.
Notes: Underused feature.

Tables
19: In the following spreadsheet:

	A	B	C
1	Animal	Quantity	Cost each (USD)
2	Sheep	20	120
3	Cows	6	100
4	Goats	15	130
5	Chickens	100	140
6	Horses	4	110

You are on cell B3. What is the first thing that happens if you select Table from the Insert ribbon?
Answer:
Excel asks you to confirm the location of data for your table, and whether your table has headers:

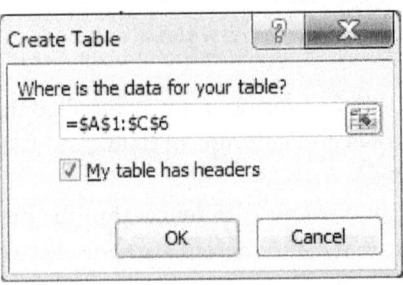

Notes: Quite often Excel will ask for additional information before performing an action.

Slicers
20: On the Insert ribbon, there is a button to insert Slicers. What are slicers?
Answer:
Slicers are easy-to-use filtering components that contain a set of buttons that enable you to quickly filter the data in a PivotTable report, without the need to open drop-down lists to find the items that you want to filter.

Notes: Slicers are new in Office 2010 - and their usage is not obvious until you have learnt them. However they are very useful.

My own commands
21: How do I add my own commands on to a ribbon?
Answer:
    a)   Go to File -> Options -> Customize Ribbon. Select the ribbon (e.g. View) and click New Group:

Advanced Excel Interview Questions You'll Most Likely Be Asked

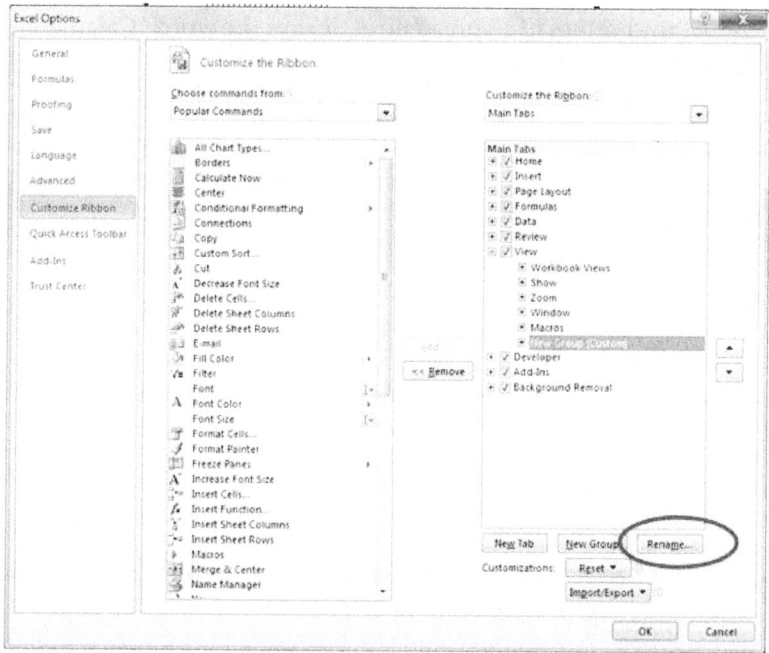

(Renaming the new group is optional)
b) Find the commands from the list and dropdown on the left and click Add to add them to the new group.
c) Click OK.

Notes: Can be used either for any standard commands or to add in any custom written macros.

Requirements
22: What are the basic hardware requirements for Excel 2010?
Answer:
a) Processor: 500 MHz or faster processor
b) Memory: 256 MB RAM or more
c) Hard disk: 2.0 GB available disk space
d) Display: 1024x576 or higher resolution monitor
e) Operating system: Windows XP (with SP3) or later

Notes: There are more requirements for some of the features to work, but these are the basic ones.

Calculations

23: At the bottom of a spreadsheet, it says the word "Calculate", like this:

What does it mean, and how can it be affected?
Answer:
It means that calculations have been set to manual for this spreadsheet. Calculations can be done either by clicking on the "Calculate" (it acts like a button) or pressing F9. It can be enabled or disabled through File -> Options -> Formulas -> Automatic; also through the options on the Formula ribbon.
Notes: Often turned ON if you have a lot of calculations and you want to change a lot of numbers. You don't need it to do all the calculations until you have finished entering the numbers. Another reason is that you have a slower computer and recalculating all the time would slow it down.

Locking cells
24: If you want to format a cell as locked:
What do you have to do the cell?
What action do you also have to take?
Answer:
You have to format the cell as Locked, from the Number, Font or Alignment dialog (on the Home ribbon) and then the Protection tab.

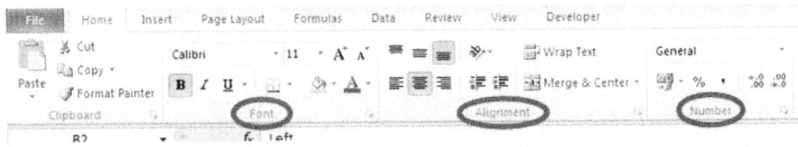

You have to protect the worksheet (review ribbon, Changes group, Protect Sheet button.
Notes: At least when you lock a cell it tells you about protecting the worksheet.

Dragging down
25: I put the year 2008 into cell A1. However when I drag down, it doesn't give me 2009, 2010 and so on but puts 2008 into every cell. How do I change it so that it gives me 2009, etc.?
Answer:
When you drag down, hold your finger on the control key. This way it will shift to incrementing the numbers.
Notes: Useful little trick, but not obvious.

Enabling Filter
26: What is the keyboard shortcut for turning on data filtering for the current area?
Answer:
The shortcut is Control-Shift-L.
Notes: Nice and quick compared with hunting through ribbons for it.

Web data
27: What does the "From Web" button do?

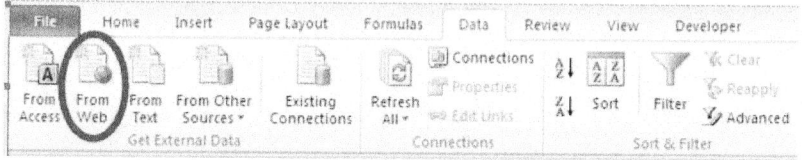

Answer:
It brings up your default web browser and allows you to import any table of data from a website, and subsequently refresh it.
Notes: You can also use this to load data from XML or HTML files on your computer.

Tips
28: What are ScreenTips, and how can you turn them ON/OFF?
Answer:
ScreenTips are small windows that display descriptive text when you rest the pointer on a command or control. They can be enabled or disabled from File -> Options -> General
Notes: These are generally useful. Thus the ability to turn them ON

or OFF is mostly used when someone has disabled them and has forgotten what they did.

Sorting

29: You have a column of data. There is a sort button that allows you to sort it into ascending order or descending order. So what does the "custom" sort do?

Answer:
It allows you to build up a multiple sort – for example sorting on gender first and then on the person's last name and then on first name. It also allows you to select whether the sort is case sensitive.

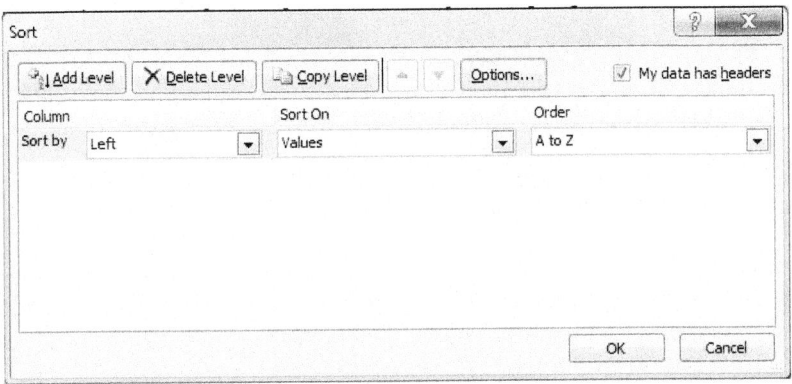

Notes: Useful when you know it, but not critical as you can always sort the data in reverse order to get the same result (in the above case it would be first name, then last name, then gender).

Keeping the headings on screen

30: You have a large spreadsheet with many rows and columns. Is it possible to keep the column headings on the screen even when you scroll down so you can still see which column is which?

Answer:
Yes. Drag the "pane" selector down from the top right and select Freeze Panes from the View menu. See the highlighted part below:

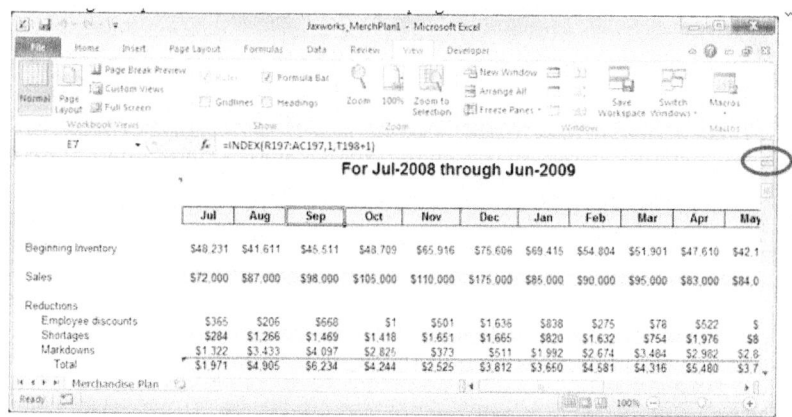

Notes: Very useful feature, especially as it stays when you save and reload.

Printing from Page 51
31: I have a document with pages from 1 to 50. I would like the spreadsheet to follow this, and thus the page numbers in the footer to count from 51. How do I set the start number for the page numbers?
Answer:
Go to Page Setup (either from the Page Layout ribbon or from File -> Print). Then set the first page number on the Page tab.
Notes: Everything else regarding the header and footer is in the Header/Footer tab of Page Setup. However the first page number is in the Page tab.

Vanishing ribbons
32: You are working on a small screen. Is there an easy way of turning off the ribbons?
Answer:
Yes. Just press Control F1.
Notes: Gives you about 5 more rows visible on the screen.

Safe mode
33: If you run Windows in Safe Mode, can you still use Microsoft Excel? Could you use previous versions of Microsoft Excel?

Answer:
Office 2010 applications will not work in Windows Safe Mode (with or without networking). This happens because the OSPP (Office Software Protection Platform) service will be disabled in Windows Safe Mode.
This does not affect the versions prior to Office 2010.
Notes: Some people either use Windows in Safe Mode because they have to, or because they like to and the loss of Excel working can be a significant impact to them.

Seeing double
34: How do I show two worksheets in the same workbook side by side?
Answer:
   a) From the View tab, select New Window. This opens a second window on the same spreadsheet.
   b) Arrange the windows (View ribbon, Arrange all) and select Vertical. Now they are side by side.
   c) On one sheet, move to the other worksheet.

Notes: Very useful, for example when you have income on one sheet and expenditure on another.

Packaging Microsoft Office
35: List which versions (e.g. Professional) of Microsoft Office 2010 come with Microsoft Excel.
Answer:
   a) Office Home and Student
   b) Office Home and Business
   c) Office Professional
   d) Office University 2010
   e) Office Standard 2010 (volume licensing version)
   f) Office Professional Plus 2010 (volume licensing version)

There are also versions in other languages and cultures. In other words, all versions of Microsoft Office come with Excel.

Notes: These do change from version to version. If someone tells you they have a version of Microsoft Office, it is worth knowing if they have Excel included or not – if they haven't used it, they may not know.

Back to front

36: You are designing a spreadsheet where it would be preferable if the column headings went down instead of up (as shown below). Is it possible to do this and, if so, how?

D	C	B	A	
				1
				2
				3

Answer:
Yes, in File -> Options -> Advanced, tick the option Show Sheet right to left. The result is like this:

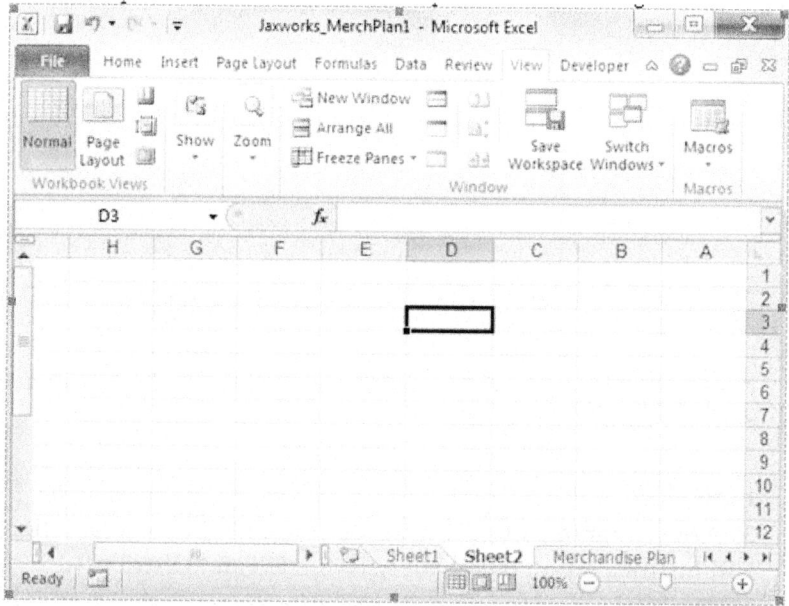

Menus using the keys

37: How is it possible to perform Menu and Ribbon options using just the keyboard, and how would you figure out which key you need for each option?

Answer:
In a cell, press the / key. Excel switches to keyboard menus and shows you the shortcut for each ribbon:

24 Advanced Excel Interview Questions You'll Most Likely Be Asked

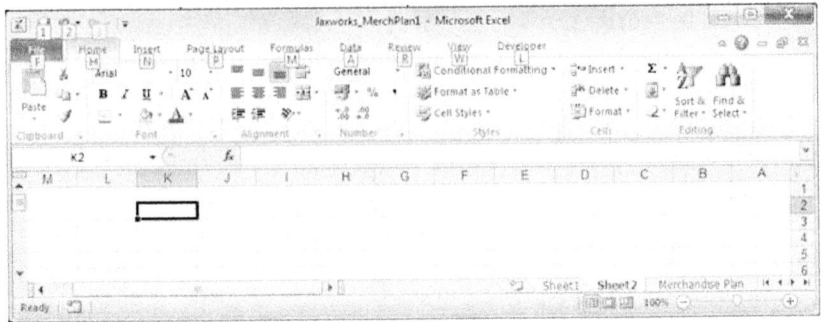

After you have pressed the key for the ribbon, Excel then shows you the keystroke(s) for each icon:

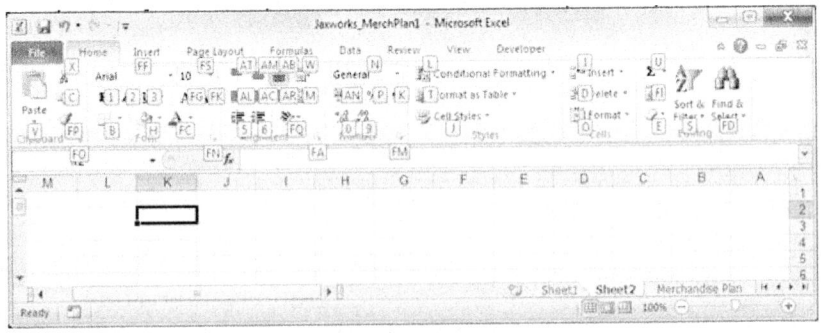

Notes: Very good if you are doing a function regularly (on different spreadsheets).

Line Up
38: When aligning text, the usual options of Left, Centered, Right and Justified are all there. But what are Fill and Distributed alignments?
For example if we have the following cells left justified,

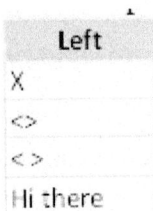

how would they appear if they were aligned using **Fill** or **Distributed**?
Answer:
Fill will fill a cell repeating the text. Distributed spreads the words across the cell.

Left	Fill	Distributed
X	XXXXXXXXX	X
<>	<><><><><>	<>
< >	< >< >< >< >	< >
Hi there	Hi there	Hi there

Notes: Can be used a separator, or to draw attention to a row.

Moving House
39: You are planning to move house, and want to create an Excel spreadsheet with all the tasks you need to do and the status of each (with probably some notes somewhere). Where do you start?
Answer:
There is an Excel template set up for this. You may want to modify it, but it is a good place to start.
Notes:
The moving house template starts like this:

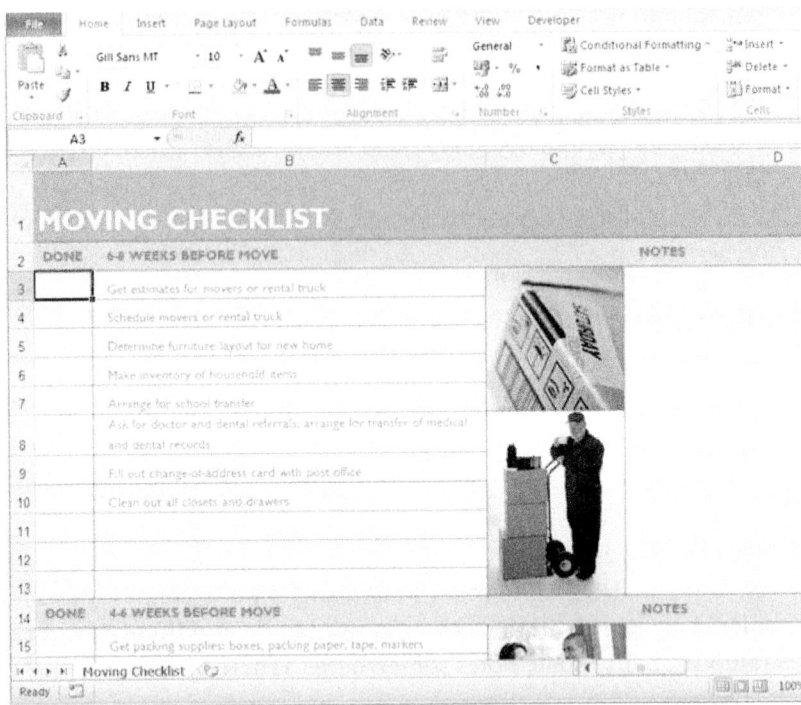

There are answers to many applications already done as templates and it is good to look through them – you never know when one will save you a lot of time (and look very professional too).

Big formulas
40: You are editing a formula and it is so long it goes off the end of the formula line. What is the keyboard shortcut for expanding the formula bar?
Answer:
To expand the formula bar, just press Control-Shift-U.
Notes: It also shrinks it. Nice feature (though not obvious) as you can do it while scrolling through your spreadsheet and you don't need to move your mouse away from the area you are looking at.

Working together
41: What sort of Excel spreadsheets can't be shared so that multiple people can open the same spreadsheet at the same time?

Answer:
Workbooks containing tables cannot be shared.
Notes: It is a useful facility. The restriction is actually identified when you hover over the Share Document button on the Review ribbon.

Just keep it plain

42: In a spreadsheet, many of the cells have been highlighted, made bold or had their colors changed as people have worked on them. I would like to bring them all back to plain black text on a white background with no bold or highlighting. What is the easiest way of doing this?

Answer:
Select all the text, either through control-A or by clicking the left of column A, as shown:

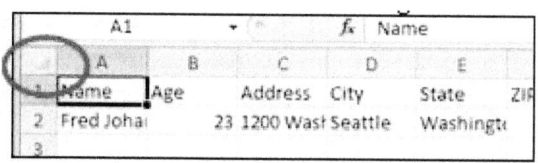

Then select the clear dropdown from the Home ribbon:

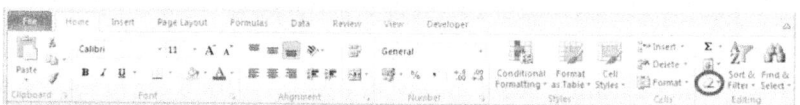

Finally select Clear Formats from the dropdown list.
Notes: The clear button may have the word "clear" next to it if the width of the Excel window is wide enough.

Balance Sheet

43: I am producing a balance sheet. All numbers I have entered are full amounts of currency, e.g. 12045.25 for $12,045.25. However the balance sheet requires all numbers to be in multiples of 1,000, so the above number would just appear as 12. How do I divide all the monetary numbers by 1,000 without creating another whole set of cells? Note I don't want the current year or other non-financial numbers divided by 12.

Answer:
Format the cells using the custom format:
#,###,
And this will do it.
Notes: The option of File -> Options -> Advanced -> Editing Options, Checking 'Automatically insert a decimal point' and selecting 3 on the spinner will divide the numbers by 1,000 – but will also divide everything on the spreadsheet which was expressly not wanted.

Lost password
44: You have a spreadsheet but have forgotten the password. What can you do?
Answer:
Firstly, some passwords just prevent editing – you may be able to view and use the spreadsheet without needing the password.
If you do need the password, do not ask Microsoft – they cannot help with lost passwords. The correct answer is to look it up on Google (or other search engine). There are lots of options on the internet that allow you to solve this (though many cost money).
Notes: When all fails, Google solves the problem. You aren't the first person with any problem as long as you can express it in generic terms.

Tutorial
45: I am printing a sheet for my students. I want them to see the row and column headings when I print my spreadsheet. How can I do this?
Answer:
The expected way is to go to Page Setup (Page Layout ribbon, or under File -> Print), go to the Sheet tab and turn on "Row and Column Headings".
Notes: You can also do it via PrintScreen and pasting into word and then printing. This will also show the ribbon and other Excel items around the screen, which may be useful for a tutorial, but wasn't specifically asked for in the question.

Too many worksheets
**46: Nearly all of my Excel workbooks are just one sheet. How do I

reconfigure Excel so that when I create a new workbook it only has 1 worksheet by default?
Answer:
In File -> Options -> General Tab, there is an option to control the number of sheets in any new Excel workbook.
Notes: This could be done through creating a template, but that is more complex to design and to implement.

Headings
47: In Word, I had styles such as Heading 1, Heading 2 and Heading 3 which I used to identify main sections in my document. Does Excel have anything similar to this?
Answer:
Yes. In the Home ribbon, there is an option called Cell Styles. The third section of the Cell Styles is Titles and Headings, and Headings 1, 2 and 3 are here.
Notes: Not as visible as they are in Word, but can still be found and used.

Column Widths
48: Some of my columns are too narrow to see all the text, while the Age column is wider than it needs to be. Give atleast two ways I can resize all my columns to fit the text.
Answer:
Method 1: Select all your data by clicking on the space above row 1 and to the left of column A, as shown:

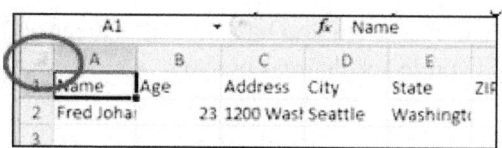

Then double click on the separator between column A and B.

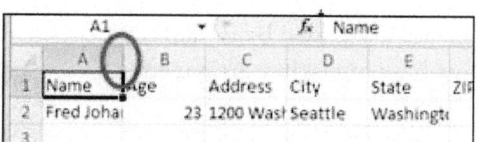

Method 2: Again select all your data, but this time select Format (on the Home ribbon) and then select Auto-Fit column width from the menu.

Method 3: Without selecting anything in particular, double click the separator between column A and B. Then repeat this across each column boundary.

Notes: Methods 1 and 2 are just different ways of doing all columns at once. Although method 3 is slower, it does allow you to select which columns are widened. For example an Address column may become so wide that the rest of the spreadsheet is not visible. It may be preferable to leave this one narrow.

Back of House
49: What is Microsoft Office Backstage and of what relevance is it to Excel?
Answer:
The backstage is where you control your spreadsheets. It is where you print your spreadsheet, export it, Options and so on. It is accessed through the File tab at the top of the ribbons.

Notes: This functionality is similar across the Office 2010 programs.

Quick formatting
50: What are the shortcut keys for formatting selected cells as either currency (e.g. $4.30) or percentage (e.g. 36%)?
Answer:
Currency is control-shift-$

Percentage is control-shift-%

Notes: Very useful when you have multiple areas of differing types as it enables you to set all areas quickly.

Automatic saving of file changes
51: How do you enable automatic saving of Excel documents and adjust how often they are saved?
Answer:
Automatic saving is enabled by default.

You can adjust how often they are saved in File -> Options -> Save:

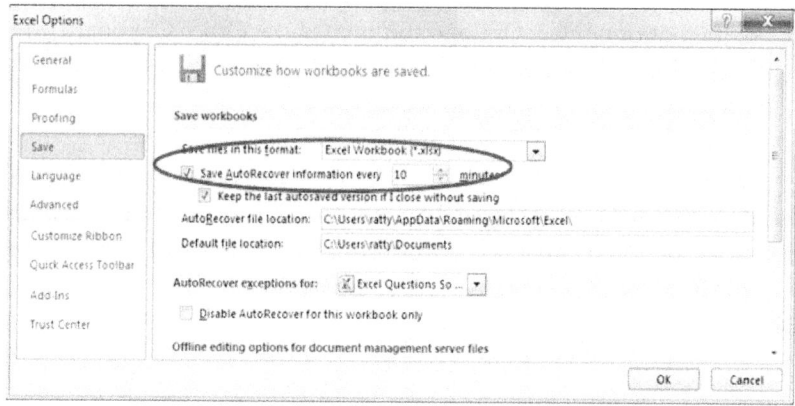

Excel functionality across 2010 versions

52: If I create a document in Microsoft Excel 2010, and then try and load it in Microsoft Excel Starter 2010, what files can load? What functionality will still work?

Answer:

All files can load and you will be able to see all the functionality from Microsoft Excel. However you can only make changes within the reduced functionality of Microsoft Excel Starter.

Notes: Files can be moved both ways without loss. In full Excel you can make all changes, in Excel starter just the basic ones.

Show Clipboard

53: You would like a key combination to be able to show the office clipboard. You could write a macro or assign a key, but what key combination does Excel offer to show you the office clipboard? As it is turned off by default, how would you enable it?

Answer:

Pressing Control-C twice.

Open the office clipboard by clicking the Clipboard arrow on the Home ribbon as shown below:

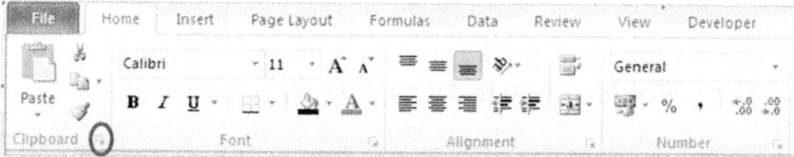

At the bottom, select Options and then Show Office Clipboard when Ctrl-C Pressed Twice.
Notes: Again not where you would expect it.

Easy reading

54: You find it easier to read text on a darker background, as shown. How can you change this within Excel and what will it affect (e.g. will it affect new spreadsheets you create)?

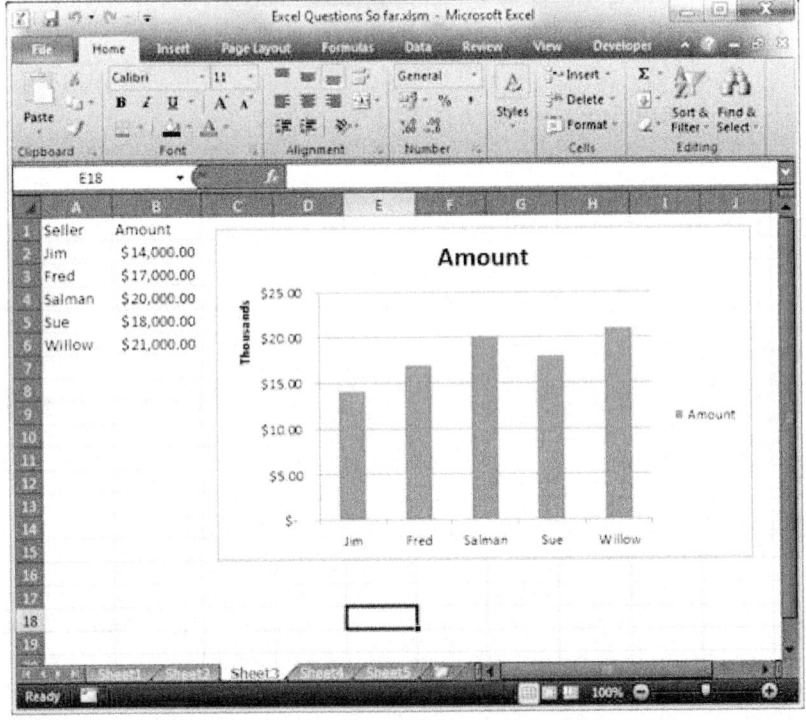

Answer:
Under File -> options -> Color Scheme. The dropdown has Black, Blue and Silver (default).
It affects everything from now on – and not only your Excel documents, but also Word and other Office applications.
Notes: More often you find it set and want to change it back.

Exporting a spreadsheet to an earlier version of Excel

55: If you want to export your spreadsheet to people who may have an earlier version of Excel, how do you find out what functionality will be lost and what may appear differently?

Answer:

There is a compatibility checker in Excel. It is found from File -> Info -> Check for Issues:

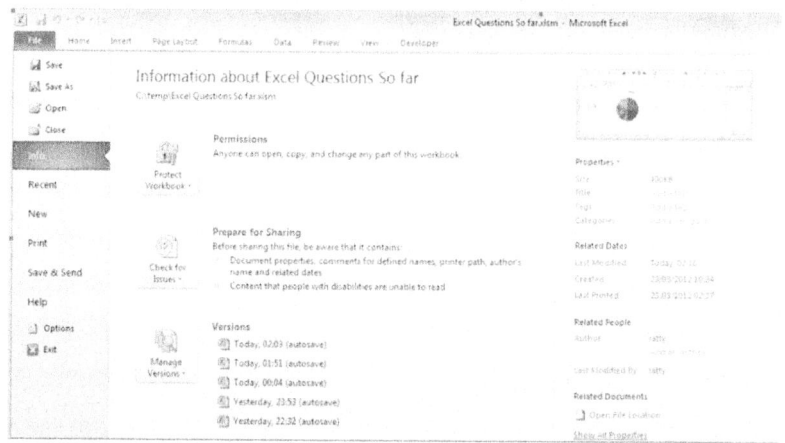

Then select the option Check Compatibility.

Notes: You will get a box like.

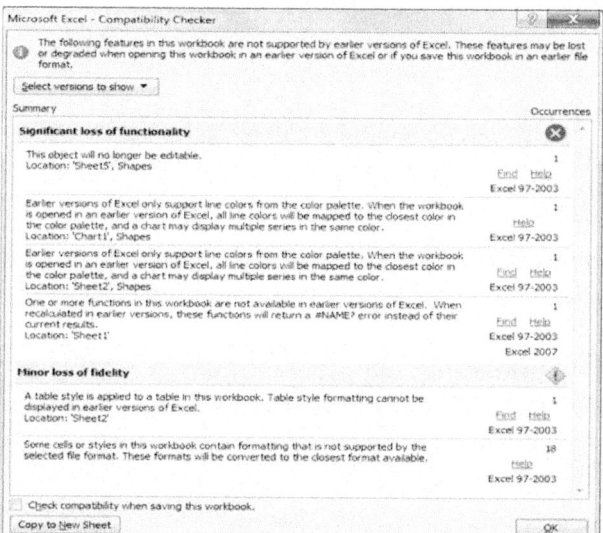

And can then decide how to address each item.

Spell Checking

56: Your company has a list of words (including the company's name) which should be accepted as valid "words" for the Excel spell checker. How can you add these words to the spell checker so it doesn't flag them every time it is used?

Answer:
Create a custom dictionary, put these words in and then add the custom dictionary to the spell checker using File -> Options -> Proofing -> Custom Dictionaries which leads to the screen shown:

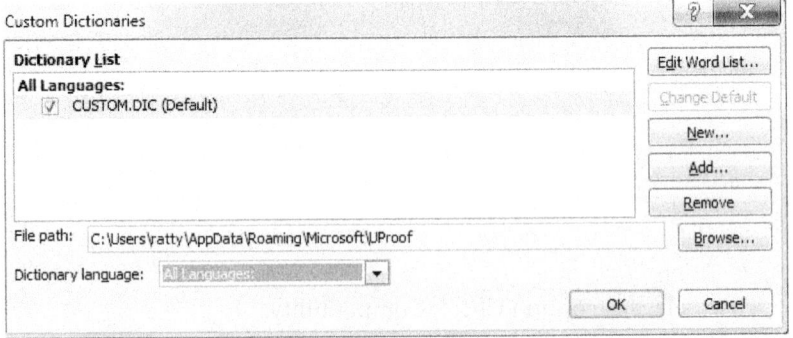

Then Add the company's dictionary.
Notes: A feature that should be used more!

Underlining

57: What is the difference between underlining and accounting underlining?

Answer:
Accounting underlining does not underline the currency symbols.
Notes: Used in producing budgets and other financial reports.

Special Formats

58: When formatting a cell, what are "Special" formats (see below)?

Advanced Excel Interview Questions You'll Most Likely Be Asked

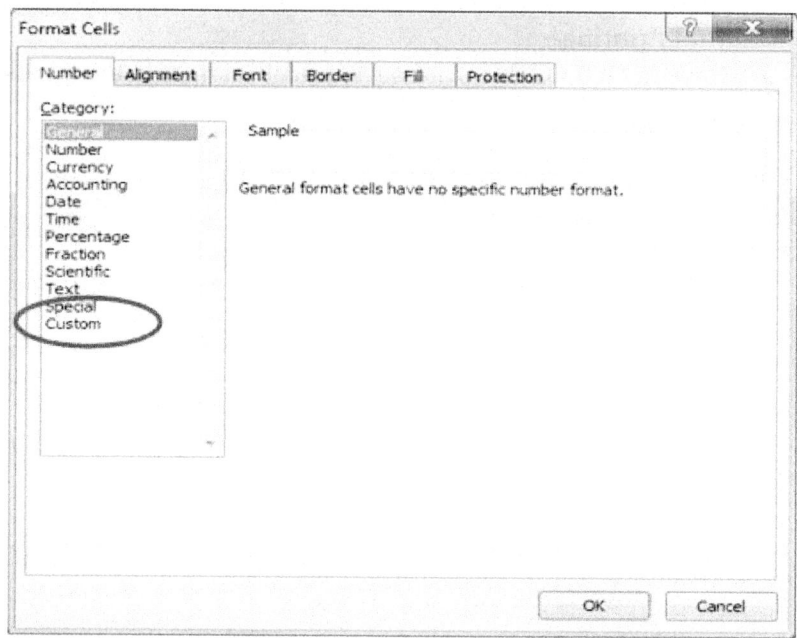

Answer:
A special format displays a number as a postal code (ZIP Code), phone number, or Social Security number.
Notes: The critical part here is that Special formats are different from custom formats.

Using the keyboard
59: If you prefer using the keyboard, what key combination moves the focus from the worksheet to get you to the ribbon and what is the sequence?
Answer:
Function key F6 does it. It cycles between:
    a) The worksheet
    b) The status bar
    c) The ribbon
    d) And back to the worksheet
Notes: When the focus is on the status bar, you can use the arrow keys to change the View and Zoom.

Central Printing

60: How do I tell Excel to print my spreadsheet right in the middle of the page?

Answer:

Firstly select the Page Setup dialog box in the Page Layout ribbon.

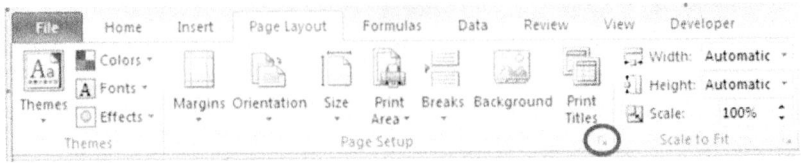

Then go to the Margins tab and select Center on page Horizontally and Vertically:

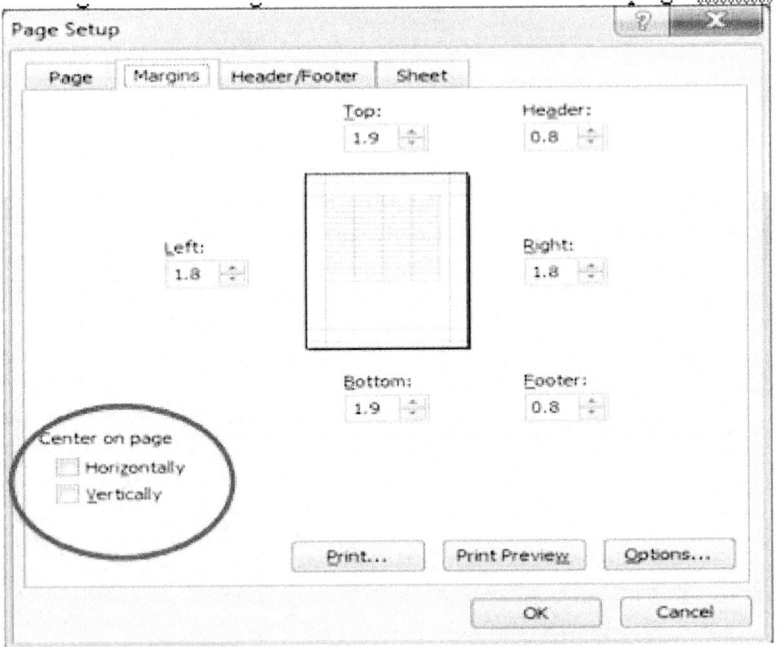

Then click OK.

Notes: For some reason, you have to go to the dialog box, despite this being a well used feature (though mostly centering horizontally rather than vertically).

Text size
61: How do you tell Excel that you want the size of the text in a cell to be small enough so that the text fits in the cell, even if the column is later made wider or narrower?
Answer:
Go to Format cells - Alignment dialog box (by clicking the small arrow to the right of Alignment at the bottom of the Home ribbon):

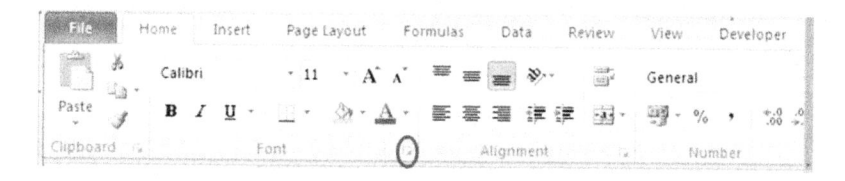

and select the option "Shrink to fit".

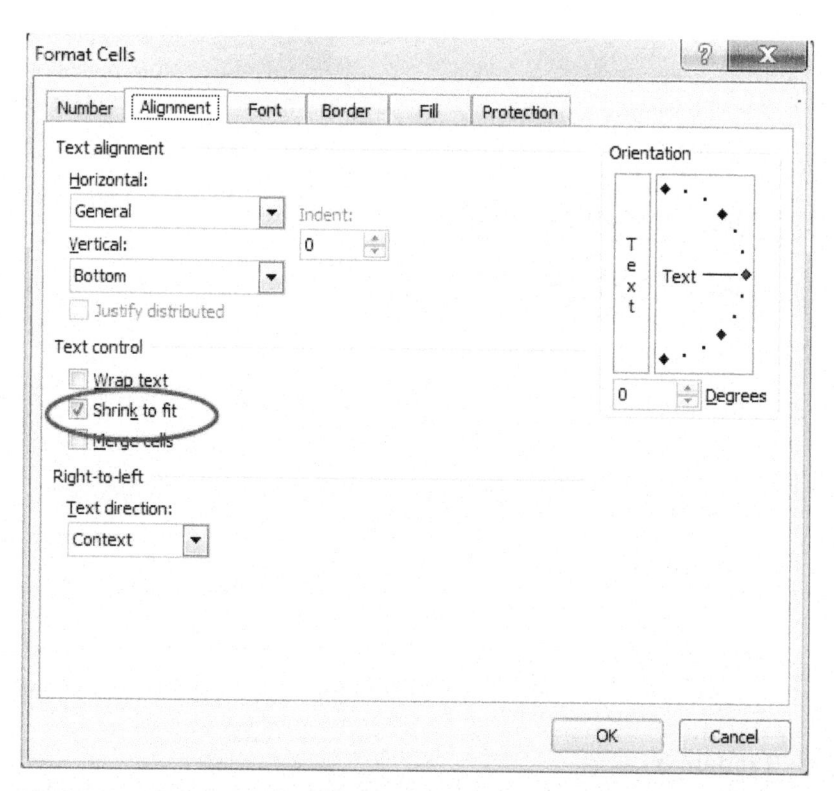

Notes: This is not on the Font tab (which controls the text size) where it would be expected. In fact there seems to be no reason why it is on the Alignment tab. But here it is. It is not made any easier by its name having nothing to do with size, font, smaller or similar words so that many help searches will not find it.

Debugging a spreadsheet

62: When debugging a spreadsheet, one factor that is useful is to highlight all cells with formulae in them. What is the quickest way of highlighting all cells with formulae in?

Answer:

This is a two-step process:
To select all cells with formulae in, go to the Find & Select dropdown on the Home ribbon and pick Formulae:

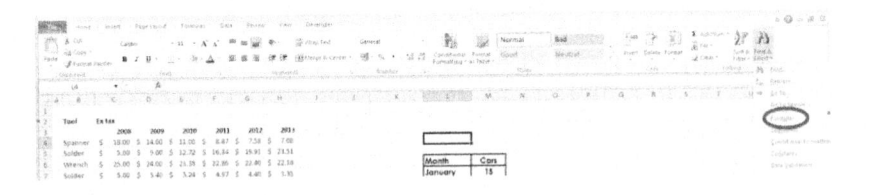

Change the cell background.

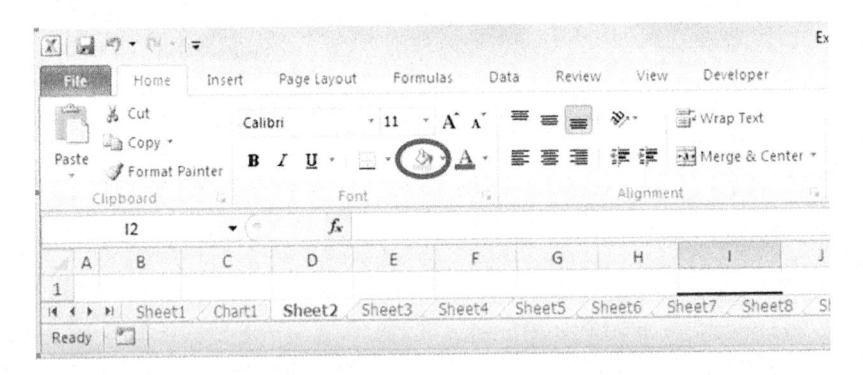

Notes: An underused feature - especially as many bugs are caused by cells that look like they are calculated but actually aren't or vice versa.

Trademarks

63: How do you put a trademark symbol after a product name in Excel (without having to go to Insert Symbol and finding it)?

Advanced Excel Interview Questions You'll Most Likely Be Asked 39

Answer:
After the product name, you type in (tm). Excel will automatically convert this to a Trademark symbol.
Notes: You can also use this for registered trademarks, euro symbols and copyright symbols.

Showing numlock and capslock
64: How do you get Excel to show if capslock or numlock is currently pressed?
Answer:
Right click on the status bar and tick the options for Caps Lock and Num Lock:

Notes: Very useful for wireless keyboards as they often don't have lights showing if Caps Lock or Num Lock are pressed.

Smile please
65: What is the camera tool, and where would you find it?
Answer:

Camera tool is your way of creating visual reference in an Excel sheet. You specify a rectangular area in your workbook and camera tool creates a mirror image of that area as a drawing object. Whenever the contents of original rectangular area change (charts, drawings or cell values) the mirror image changes too. The camera tool is not on any ribbon. You can either access it by adding it to the Quick Access toolbar or by adding it to a custom group on a ribbon.

Notes:
It is one of the useful and hidden features of Excel. It was more accessible in earlier versions.

Formulae

The ability to put in a formula to address a specific requirement

Conditional formulae

66:

	A	B	C
1	Animal	Quantity	Cost each (USD)
2	Sheep	20	120
3	Cows	6	100
4	Goats	15	130
5	Chickens	100	140
6	Horses	4	110

In the above spreadsheet you decide to write an array formula to find the total cost of all the animals. What is the formula you would use and how would you identify to Excel that it is an array formula?
Answer:
The formula is
=sum(B2:B6*C2:C6)
NB: Also accept
{=sum(B2:B6*C2:C6)}
as this is how it appears on the screen
It is identified to Excel by pressing Control + Shift + Enter after typing it in.
Notes: Array formulae often save an entire column of intermediate calculations, but are little known.

Times

67: With the sheet shown below, what is the simplest formula to work out the number of seconds elapsed between the date and time that the process started and when it ended?

	A	B	C
1		Date	Time
2	Process started	2/4/2012	1:36 am
3	Process ended	3/4/2012	2:18 pm

Answer:
=(B3+C3-B2-C2)*24*60*60
Notes: Excel stores all dates internally in days. So all we have to do is add B3+C3 to get the end, subtract B2+C2 (the start) and then

multiply by 24 hours in a day, 60 minutes in an hour and 60 seconds in a minute.

True or False
68: With reference to the above table, what would you get from the following formulae?
=A1+A2+A3
and
=sum(A1:A3)
Answer:
With
=A1+A2+A3
You would get the value of 2.
And with
=sum(A1:A3)
You get the number 0.
Notes: You have to be very careful when dealing with values of TRUE and FALSE. It is often the case that you want to count how many TRUE's there are, and just adding the numbers up can get the wrong answers.

Vlookup
69: In the below spreadsheet:

	A	B
1	ProductID	Name
2	120	Bread
3	121	Butter
4	122	Margerine

If I have a cell (D4) with 121 in it, I can use vlookup to give me the product's name. The question is if the cell D4 has the name of the product (e.g. "Butter"), how do I write the formula to find the product's ID?
Answer:
=INDEX(A1:A3,MATCH(D4,B1:B3,0))
Notes: $ signs can be added before any of the cells, so for A1 (for

example), A$1, $A1 and $A$1 are also right. The catch here is that vlookup only goes from left to right. So although you are planning to use vlookup, that function won't work at all from right to left. You have to use a completely different formula.

In third place...

70: In my local league, the score of each person is recorded. As the scoring system works, no two people can have the same score. I want the spreadsheet to identify who is currently in first, second and third place. Thus I want a formula to go into B2 (which can be dragged down to B4 without changing it) to give me the names of who is currently in each place. What is the simplest formula to do it?

	A	B
1	Place	Person
2	First	
3	Second	
4	Third	
5		
6	Score	Person
7	125	James
8	209	Jill
9	133	Jeremy
10	217	Jamal
11	179	John
12	211	Jessica

Answer:
=VLOOKUP(LARGE(A$7:A$12,ROW()-1),A$7:B$12,2,FALSE)

Notes: Firstly, the row function tells us which row we are in. As the rows 2, 3 and 4 are used for first, second and third place, we need row()-1 for the place. Then large will tell us what the score is for that place, for example =large(range,3) will give the third largest number in that range. Fortunately we have no draws here. Finally, vlookup will tell us the name. Note the false at the end as the numbers are not in ascending order. This tests a simple question with quite a complex answer. However the answer can be done in each cell without needing intermediate cells.

Absolute, not relative
71: You have a spreadsheet like this:

	A	B	C
1	Item	Base price	Tax
2	Spanner	$15.00	=B2*B5
3	Wrench	$18.00	
4			
5	Tax Rate	10%	

You are typing in a formula into cell C2 for the tax. You realize that when you click on the cell B5 for the tax, Excel put in a relative cell reference instead of the absolute one you really wanted as you plan to drag this formula down the column. What is the easiest way to convert this reference in B5 to an absolute reference?
Answer:
Just press the function key F4 and Excel will change the relative cell reference B5 to the absolute reference $B$5 for you.
Notes: The obvious answer from the user is for the user to say that you need $ signs. Though this is correct that you need dollar signs, the question asked is what is the easiest way to put them in and the answer given does it for you.

Formula error
72: Is there anything wrong with this formula and, if so, what is it?
=IF(A1<40,"Fail",IF(AND(A1>400,A1<70),"Pass","Merit"))
Answer:
If A1 is exactly 40, the result will be a Merit, which is clearly not intended.
Notes: Spotting errors in formulae is difficult. Especially when the error will only occur in one specific example.

Reading Formulae 1
73: What does the following formula do?
=SUBSTITUTE(IF(RIGHT(TRIM(A1))="-

",RIGHT(TRIM(A1))&A1,A1),"-","",2)+0
Answer:
Basically it looks for negative numbers where the minus sign is on the right and replaces it with a number with the minus sign on the left.
Notes: The format of "100-" comes from a range of packages, for example SAP. Having imported it, it is needed to swap the "100-" for "-100".

Sorting
74: Working with the following spreadsheet (on sheet1):

	A	B	C
1	3	=A1	=Sheet1!A1
2	2	=A2	=Sheet1!A2
3	1	=A3	=Sheet1!A3

As you would expect, it displays as:

	A	B	C
1	3	3	3
2	2	2	2
3	1	1	1

The question is: How will it display after you have sorted column 1 (into ascending order)?
Answer:

	A	B	C
1	1	1	3
2	2	2	2
3	3	3	1

Notes: This is one that can cause a bug in your spreadsheet. Depending on whether you specify the sheet name affects how it sorts. So two apparently identical formulae act differently after sorting.

BAHTTEXT
75: What does the following formula do?
=BAHTTEXT(12.3)

Answer:

Technically, you get

หนึ่งร้อยยี่สิบสามบาทถ้วน

What the formula does is converts the number into text and then displays it, so this represents "one hundred twenty three baht". (yes, it does add the word Baht on the end). Finally it converts the text into Thai (as spoken in Thailand).

Notes: One of the strangest functions in Excel because it actually converts numbers into text. For anyone who has not either lived in Thailand or worked with Thai people this is a very difficult question!

Precedents

76: In Excel, what are precedents, and how do you get to see them?
Answer:

Precedents allow you to see what cells or areas were used in deriving the value in a particular cell. You can invoke it from Trace Precedents on the Formulas tab.

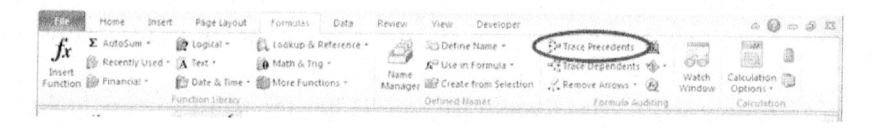

For example in the sheet below:

The cell D3 has a formula that draws information from the cell B3 and from the area G8:H14, as shown by the arrows.
Notes: This question is deliberately written the "wrong way round". Normally you are presented with a problem and want to use Excel to solve it and thus are searching for the solution. Here you are given the solution and asked what problem it addresses. In real life, there are times when you be asked by someone what that functionality does and they look to you for a solution. The Trace Precedents and Trace Dependents are very useful in tracking down errors or understanding someone else's spreadsheets.

Finding Words

77: The Find function allows you to find a set of characters in a cell, for example to find "jumps" in "the quick brown fox jumps over the lazy dog". However what if you are searching for a word and don't want your formula to pick it up in another word. For example "pen" in "the pen is mighty" will be found but it will not trigger in "metalwork and carpentry". You can't guarantee that there are spaces round it as there may be punctuation marks around. How do you find if the word you are looking for is there?
Assume cell A1 has the phrase and B1 has the word you are looking for, what do you put into C1 to show if B1 is a word in A1?

	A	B	C
1	The pencil and pen.	Pen	

Answer
=ExactWordInString(A1,B1)
Notes: There is a function that does what you want - don't try writing one yourself!

Starting off

78: What formula would find all cells in the named range "data" where the value starts with the letter "t" or "T"?
Answer:
=COUNTIF(data,"t*")
Notes: The "countif" function is not case sensitive.

Maxis and Minis

79: You had a formula to average the set of students' marks, which was:

=average(marks)

However you now want to discard the lowest and highest marks and just average the rest. What formula would you now use?

Answer:

=(sum(marks)-min(marks)-max(marks))/(count(marks)-2)

Notes: Note that average can't drop the highest and lowest so you need to do it in another way. Note also that you have to divide by count()-2 as you now have two fewer values.

Value errors

80: In the spreadsheet below, a formula was put into cell D2 and dragged down. What reason(s) could there be for the cell D3 showing an error?

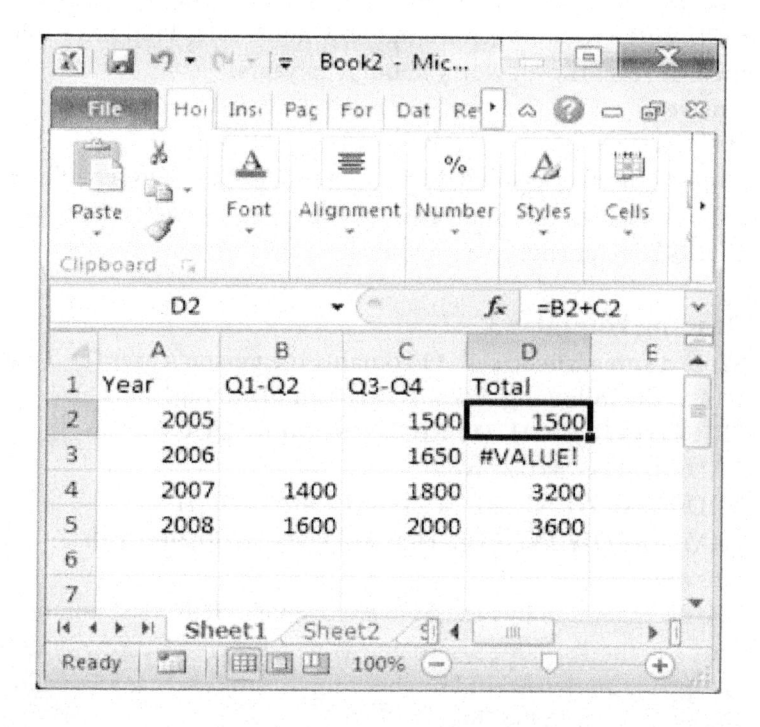

	A	B	C	D	E
1	Year	Q1-Q2	Q3-Q4	Total	
2	2005		1500	1500	
3	2006		1650	#VALUE!	
4	2007	1400	1800	3200	
5	2008	1600	2000	3600	

Answer:

The cell B3 contains text (possibly by someone typing a single quote into the cell followed by a space). Excel cannot add text to a number and thus issues an error.
Notes: Cell B2 was left completely empty. Excel is happy with this and treats it as 0 for the purpose of the addition.

Countifs
81: With the following spreadsheet:

	A	B	C
1	Salesman	Date	Amount
2	Fred	1/3/12	$100
3	Jill	1/4/12	$120
4	Fred	1/5/12	$50

And so on down columns A, B and C (the last row will keep changing as more data are added). How would you write the COUNTIFS formula to find out how much sales Fred has made in the last year? (Don't worry about leap years)
Answer:
=COUNTIFS(A:A,"Fred",B:B,">="&TODAY()-365)
Notes: This is a combination of using A:A to represent the whole column, today()-365 to measure the last year as well as the use of the COUNTIFS function.

Reading Formulae 3
82: In a spreadsheet, cell A1 contains the person's user ID. Then cell B1 has the following. What is this formula doing?
=RIGHT(A1)=RIGHT(10-RIGHT(SUMPRODUCT(--MID("01234567891x3x5x7x9",
MID(A1,ROW(INDIRECT("1:"&(LEN(A1)-1))),1)*
(1+MOD(ROW(INDIRECT("1:"&(LEN(A1)-1))),2))+1,1))))
Answer
The usernames in this example are people's credit card numbers. The formula checks if the username is a valid credit card number. An acceptable answer would be checking that the username is valid.
Notes: There are clues here:
From the middle "=", it is doing a calculation which returns a logical

answer (true or false). Thus checking the username is valid is a logical step.

RIGHT(A1) gives the last digit, so the last digit is being compared against the rest of the digits. This would also lead you to a check digit.

The answer happens to be the formula for credit cards, but it would take some wading through to notice this.

Weekdays

83: I have imported some data and column A has the dates in. I have inserted a new column to the left and want to put the day of the week into it. What's the simplest way of doing this?

	A	B
1		Date
2	Thursday	2/2/2012
3	Friday	2/3/2012

and so on.

Answer:
 a) In cell A2, put the formula:
    B2
 b) Drag down the column
 c) Format the column using the conditional format "dddd"

Notes: Using Excel's inbuilt facility for the names of the days saves typing them in, and just using the format saves even working them out. Although the answer is easy, there are many other, much longer ways of doing this. The easiest way is usually the best.

Putting in returns in a cell

84: You want to put into cell B1 "House Prices 2012". To ensure it wraps correctly, you want to put a return into the cell (to have 2 lines of text in the cell). Is it possible and, if so, how?

	A	B
1		House Prices 2012

Answer:
It is possible. After the first line, press ALT+ENTER and then you can type the second line.
Notes: Obviously could be done in 2 rows, but if you wanted this in every cell, having 2 rows makes filtering and sorting much harder. So having it in one row can be important.

Taking returns out of cells
85: In a spreadsheet, there is column A with cities and states in them. The person has them on 2 lines with a line break between them. You want to convert them to the format "City, State". What formula do you put into B1 (and then drag down) to do this?

	A	B
1	Richmond Virginia	
2	San Diego California	
3	Fort Wayne Indiana	

Answer
=SUBSTITUTE(A1,CHAR(10),", ")
Notes: The key here is that Excel stores a line break as CHAR(10) and then you can use the substitute function.

Clean and tidy
86: What does the CLEAN() function do?
Answer:
It removes all nonprintable characters from text (ASCII 0 to 31).
Notes: Bit of a strange one as it's not obvious from its name.

Understanding formulae 4
87: What does the following formula do?
{=(SUM(LEN(Data))-
SUM(LEN(SUBSTITUTE(Data,Text,""))))/LEN(Text)}

Answer:
It counts the number of occurrences of a string (Text) within a range of cells (Data).

Notes: If you change all occurrences of Text in Data to nothing, the string gets shorter by the length of the text times the number of occurrences. Thus dividing by the length of the text gives the number of occurrences.

Spaced Out
88: A column has text in it that is not lined up. You have tracked it down to the fact that there a variable number of spaces in front of the text in each cell. If the cells affected are A1 to A200, what formula would you put into cell A2 (and then drag down) to get rid of these spaces?
Answer:
=trim(A1)

Notes: Actually the answer is very easy – if you know it. If not, you could have a long formula on your hand with multiple replaces or more.

Sum error
89: In the following spreadsheet, why is the sum at the bottom of the column showing 0?

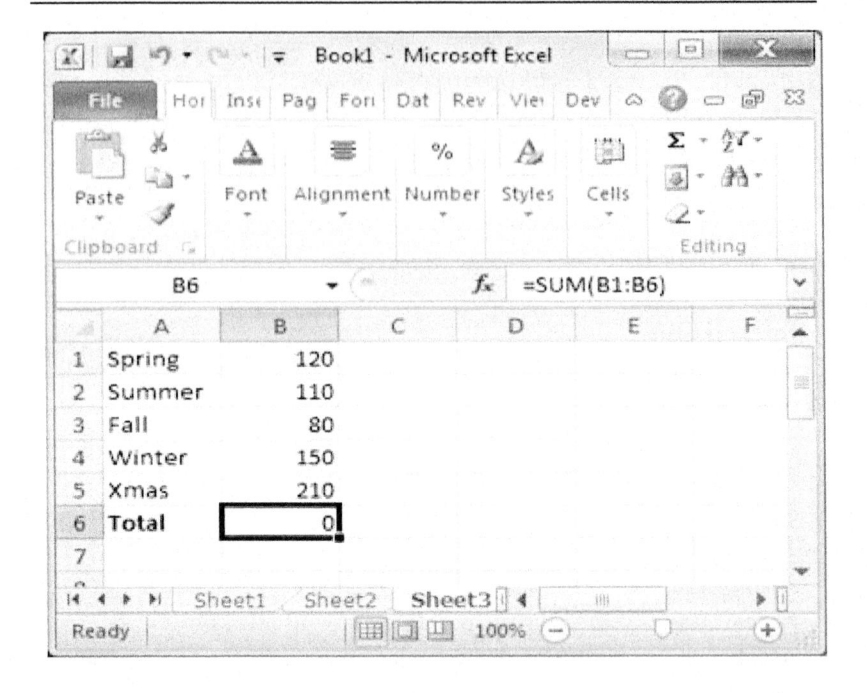

Answer:
Because the formula in cell B6 includes a reference to the cell B6 itself, creating a circular reference.

Notes: Circular references do flag up when they are created. However if they are ignored, they can lead to false results (as shown) and not be easy to track down.

Referring to cells on other sheets
90: On my spreadsheet, the first worksheet is called "Raw Data". On cell A1 on sheet 2, how do I say that the contents of this cell should be the same as that on cell A1 on the first sheet?

Answer:
='Raw Data'!A1

Also there could be $ signs before the A or 1 or both, e.g.
='Raw Data'!$A$1

Notes: This is both a test of the exclamation mark for other sheets and what happens if there is a space in the name of the other sheet.

Formula Error

91: In the following spreadsheet:

	A	B	C	D
1	Chicago	Illinois	USA	

What is wrong with the following formula for the cell D1?
=concatenate(A1,B1,C1)
Answer:
As a formula, it is correct. However it will leave no spaces between the items, so you will get:
ChicagoIllinoisUSA
Notes: When checking formulae, not all problems will generate error messages.

Calculations on nothing

92: Is it possible to get Excel to tell you whenever you have entered a formula that uses a cell which is empty?
Answer:
Yes. In File -> Options -> Formulas, there is a tick box for "Formulas referring to empty cells".
Notes: Can be useful when the cells you are calculating on are on another worksheet and thus not visible.

Working time

93: You have the exact time for an event in cell A1. What formula would you write to round this time to the nearest 15 minutes?
Answer:
Either
=ROUND(A1*24/0.25,0)*(0.25/24)
Or
=ROUND(A1*96,0)/96
which is just a rewrite of the first formula
Notes:
A1*24 turns A1 from hours to days.
A1*24/0.25 does the same, but for quarter hours (hence the 0.25)
=ROUND(A1*24/0.25,0) then rounds it off, and finally
=ROUND(A1*24/0.25,0)*(0.25/24) turns it back to quarter hours.

Understanding formulae 6
94: What does the following formula do?
=MONTH(DATE(YEAR(A1),2,29))=2
Answer:
It finds out whether the date entered into cell A1 is a leap year.
Notes: The formula works out which year that the date is in, and then the date function puts together a date with the 29th of February in this year. The way the date function works is that if the number of days is more than there are in the month, it wraps into the next month. Thus, if it is not a leap year, the 29th will wrap into March. So if we just check if the 29th has caused the month to wrap, we have checked if it's a leap year.

Viewing formulas
95: You have a complex spreadsheet, not huge but many calculations all over the place. How is it possible to show the original formulae in the cells rather than the numbers that they calculate?
Answer:
Press Control-` (key at the top left of the keyboard, besides 1) to switch.
Notes: Often one that if someone has accidentally done, it can be useful to know how to switch off. Note that the solution will depend on the keyboard. On a Spanish keyboard, for example, you would press control ~, where ~ is found above the n key.

Only calculate if needed
96: I want to calculate the results of adding C4 and C5 and then multiplying the result by C6, but only if there is some data in cells C2, C4 and B1. What is the formula for doing this?
Answer:
=IF(AND(C2<>"",C4<>"",B1<>""),(C4+C5)*C6,"")
Notes: Often questions are posed in text form. The objective is to work out what is needed. Note the brackets around (C4+C5). These are crucial otherwise the multiplication will be done before the addition.

Decades

97: How do you change all years to show which decade they are in? For example:

	A	B
1	Year	Decade
2	1939	1930
3	1942	1940
4	1945	1940
5	1950	1950

Just give the formula for cell B2, in a form that can be dragged down to B5.
Answer:
=floor(A2,10)
Notes:
Quick and easy. That the normal rounding functions don't do it as they will round 1939 up to 1940. You could do it through:
=int(A2/10)*10
But this is more complex than needed - especially when Excel specifically provides a function for it.

Breaking down a formula
98: A complex sheet has a cell with a long formula in cell C4 (with filled cells al around). How do you break down the formula to figure out what it is doing?
Answer:
Use the Evaluate Formula button on the Formulas Ribbon.

Division by zero
99: If I have a formula in C1 that divides one number by another:
=B1/A1
I could test if A1 was 0 and then only divide if it is non-zero.
However I actually have a much more complex formula with many divisions, any one of which could generate the error. So the question is, how do I write a (short) formula for the first example

which does not have to check if A1 is zero before doing the calculation?
Answer:
=IFERROR(A1/B1,0)
Notes: Also this is faster than writing code to test for zero and then doing the division.

Month length
100: Cell A1 has a date. What formula would be needed to return the number of days in the month that A1 falls. For example if A1 had January 10th, 1993; the result would be 31, because January 1993 had 31 days.
Answer:
=DAY(DATE(YEAR(A1),MONTH(A1)+1,0))
Notes: The date function converts a day, month and year to a date. If we put a 0 in the day, that's the 0th day. Excel knows that the first of a month is day 1, so the 0th must be the day before, i.e. the last day of the previous month. So we add one to the month (making it one month later) and then ask Excel to give us the last day of the month before. For example if we had January 10th 1993, we would ask Excel to give us the date for February 0th 1993, which Excel would work out to 31st January 1993. Then we apply the day() function to just give us the day part (dropping the January 1993).

Showing distances
101: I have a column which shows the height or ornaments to the nearest inch. They are currently numbers converted from centimetres, e.g. 14.803. I would like them displayed to the nearest whole number followed by the inch sign, e.g. 15". How do I do this?
Answer:
Use the following custom format:
0\"
Notes
The 0 makes it a whole number, the " means inches and the backquote \ tells Excel not to take the quote mark as the start of text but to take it literally.

Named ranges
102: I have a named range that is defined like this:
=OFFSET(Sheet1!$A$2,0,0,COUNTA(Sheet1!$A:$A)-1)
What area does it refer to?
Answer:
It is the cells from A2 down to the end of the column (however many cells it is).
Notes: Especially used for graphs as it will auto update if more data is added.

Tutorials
103: I am looking for low cost online tutorials for Microsoft Excel. Where is a good place to start looking?
Answer:
You could start with searching the internet. However many of the courses are either expensive or poor quality. The best place to start is on the Microsoft web site, where they offer tutorials in a range of topics on Excel, all free.
office.microsoft.com/en-us/excel-help/getting-started-with-excel-2010-HA010370218.aspx
Notes: There is much that Microsoft does not offer. But when it does, it is worth knowing about as it is often reliable and well-presented information and in some cases (like tutorials) free.

Vlookup failing
104: You have written a formula including the function vlookup, but it isn't working as expected. Give three possible reasons for this
Answer:
Any three of the following:
    a) The data are not sorted properly
    b) The value sought comes before the first range
    c) There is no matching data found in the lookup table
    d) There is a mismatch in the data type
    e) There are extraneous spaces in the cells or code
    f) There are special characters in the cells, for example tab, linefeed, carriage return, or a non-breaking space
    g) Vlookup is not case sensitive

Lowest quickly

105: I have a column and want to find the lowest number. Is there a button in Excel which will do this for me?

Answer:

Yes. The Autosum button on the Home tab offers minimum, maximum, average and count numbers as well as the sum (that you would expect):

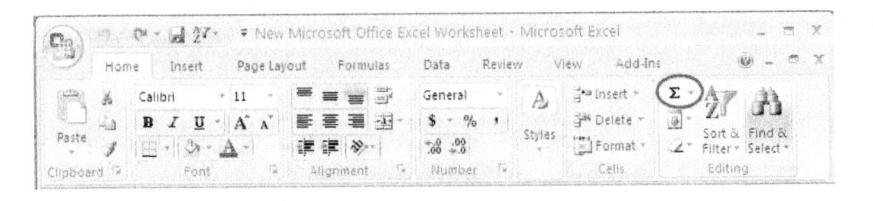

The same Autosum dropdown is also on the functions tab:

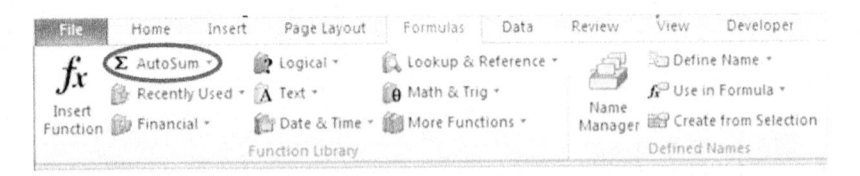

Notes: This is one of the functions that an experienced Excel programmer would never even look at. He would find is quicker to type in:

=min(A2:A7)

However if he is teaching someone else, having the function in a list is easy and saves having to remember that for lowest value, the function is called min.

Function help

106: You are working out interest payments and have selected the function PMT (as shown below), but need to look something up in the Help system. What is the quickest way of finding Help on this function?

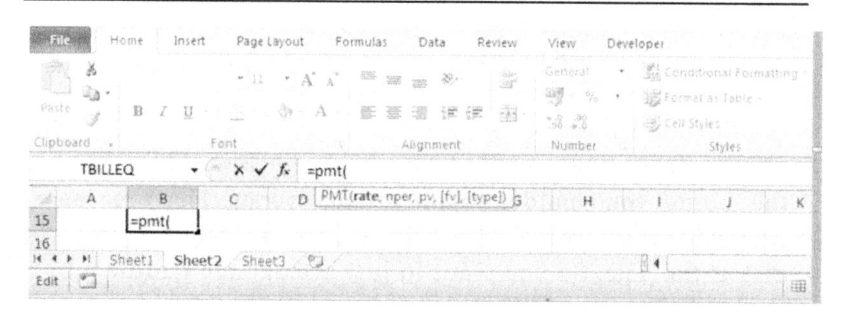

Advanced Excel Interview Questions You'll Most Likely Be Asked   61

Answer:
Just click on the function name in the tool tip, as shown:

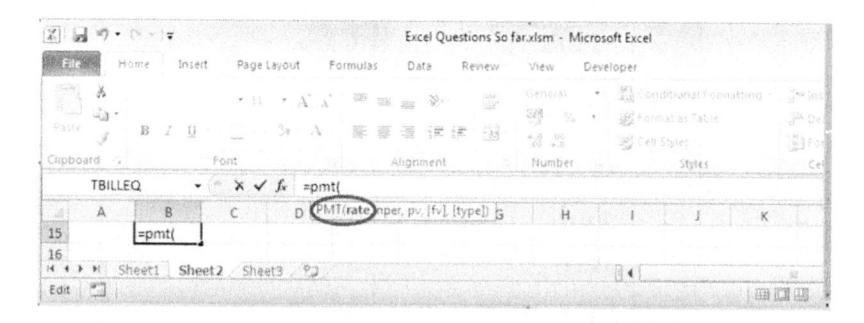

Notes: This is very useful.

One formula for multiple cells
107: You have a spreadsheet and you want to add a formula to the bottom of each column that averages all the values.
You select the empty row that the formula is going to go in and type in the formula for the first column:
=average(A2:A7)
What is the easiest way to get this one formula to be applied to all the columns?
Answer:
Instead of pressing Enter, press Control+Enter and this will do it for you.
Notes: There are many other ways, such as:
  a) Dragging right
  b) Fill right
  c) Control-r

d) But the question asked for the easiest way.

All middle values
108: You have a spreadsheet like the one below. At the bottom of the column you would normally put the average. However there are occasions when there could be an extreme value which would distort the data. So you want to just average the middle numbers (i.e. excluding the highest and lowest number). What formula do you use (for cell B8)?

	A	B
1	Month	Cars
2	January	15
3	February	17
4	March	32
5	April	16
6	May	9
7	June	14
8	Average	

Answer:
=(SUM(L7:L12)-MAX(L7:L12)-MIN(L7:L12))/(COUNT(L7:L12)-2).
Notes: Just add up them all, subtract the highest and lowest and then divide by 2 less than the count of how many numbers you have.

Editing in cell and in the formula bar
109: If you are on a cell with a formula, what key would you normally press to edit the formula in the cell? Also, what would happen if this key does not work and, instead takes you to the formula bar?
Answer:
The key you press is the function key F2.
If it takes you to the formula bar, then in-cell editing has been disabled. You can re-enable it by going to the File menu -> Options -> and tick the box labeled "Allow editing directly in cells":

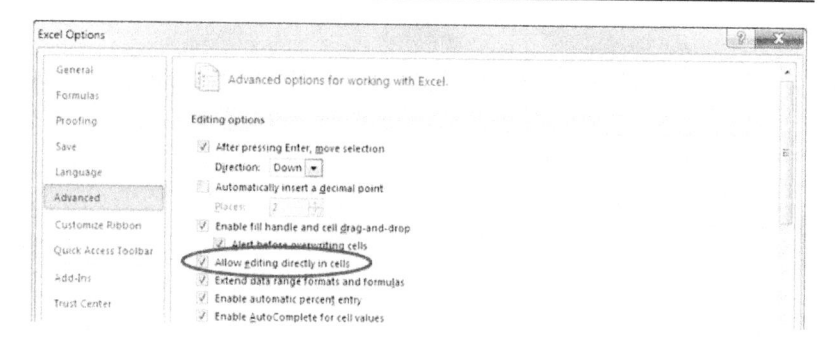

Advanced Excel Interview Questions You'll Most Likely Be Asked

Notes: Unlikely to be turned off, but once it is, it is useful to know where to find it to turn it back on again. You may assume it has something to do with the keyboard, shortcuts or other area and this is not an obvious place for it.

Holidays
110: I have the following spreadsheet:

	A	B
1	Today	1 June 2012
2	Deadline	30 September 2012
3	Working days	

where all dates are entered as dates (not as text).
Our company works on Mondays to Fridays only. I want to find the number of working days between today and the deadline. In addition, the company will close on Monday 17th to Tuesday 18th September for its national conference, and also Wednesday the 4th of July and the first Monday in September are national holidays.
What formula do I put into cell B3?
Answer:
=NETWORKDAYS(B1,B2)-4
Notes: The function networkdays() works out how many weekdays there are between the dates. The national holidays and the conference dates are all weekdays. So we just need to subtract 4 for these four days. There is no need to work out what date labor day (first Monday in September) actually falls on. We know it is on a Monday and is definitely within the period, so we can just subtract 1 day for it.

Shift working

111: I work on shifts, taking Tuesday and Wednesdays off each week. What formula do I use to find out how many days there are from now to the end of December (just put the current year in)? Note that the current date will change, so we will need the function for this as well.

Answer:
=networkdays.intl(now(),date(2012,12,31),4)

Notes:
Now() gives us today.
Date(2012,12,31) gives us the end of December (in this case in 2012).
The option 4 means we are taking Tuesdays and Wednesdays off. Fortunately Excel offers us a list so we don't have to remember that Tuesdays and Wednesdays are number 4.

Edate

112: What does the function edate() do?

Answer:
edate() adds specified number of months to a given date.
For example, if A1 has 6/6/2011, edate(A1,4) will give 10/6/2011 (US format).
Notes: This is an odd one in that it only adds months. There is no option to add days, weeks, quarters, years, etc. The date() function does the date, and also supports years and days.

Problems

The ability to solve "real world" problems in Excel, where even the approach may not be obvious

Chessboard

113: Using just a single conditional format, how do you create a chessboard pattern of alternating black and white cells?

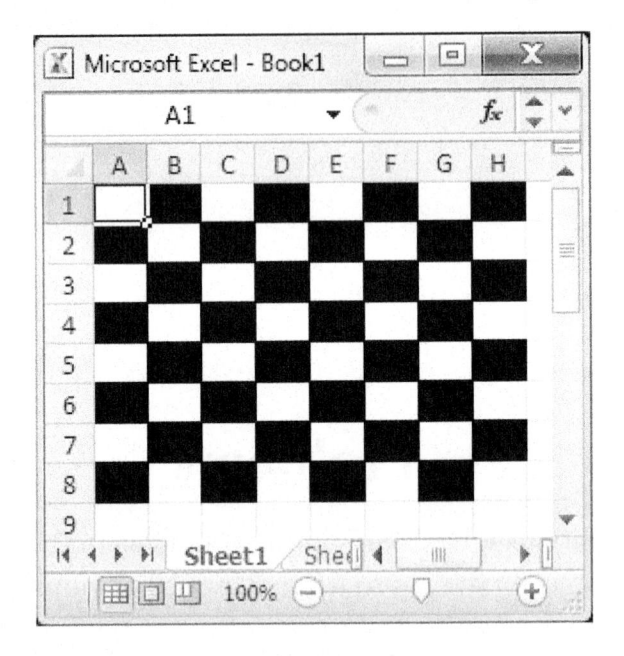

Answer:
Clearly there may be more than one way of doing it. However a simple answer is:
Conditional Format rule: Use this formula:
=mod(row()+column(),2)=1
OR
=iseven(row()+column())
Format: background set to Black
Notes: The formula ensures that the white cells have nothing in them (so you don't see the number 0 in every white cell).
The formula:
=isodd(row()+column())
will also work, but will make the top left cell black (instead of white as in the picture) which is why it wasn't given as an answer).
Notes: People use Excel for a wide range of tasks. Often just to create something to print without actually doing any calculations at all (e.g.

a form or a table).

Calendar
114: You want to use Excel to create a calendar for next year, with your photos above each month. How would you do this?
Answer:
There is a template that does this for you. All you need do is enter the year and change the pictures (if necessary).

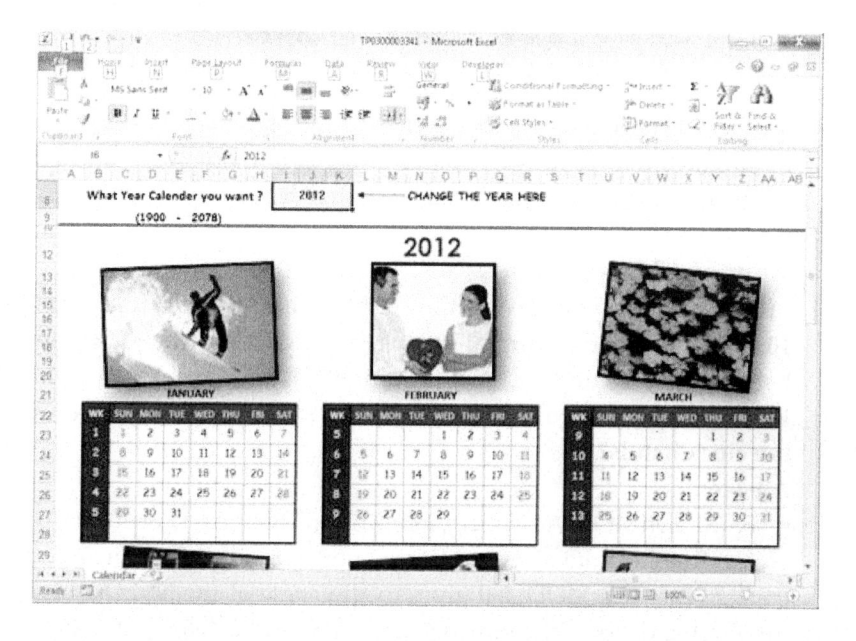

Notes: This is not a question testing whether you know every template. The question should be looked at as "I want to do something that lots of people would want to do in Excel". That would take you to the templates. There are several calendar templates and any one of them would do and could be modified to suit.

Full stops and commas in numbers
115: You live in a country where a comma shows thousands and a full stop is the decimal point. For example 1234½ would be shown as 1,234.5.
However you have been sent a comma separated text file from Spain, where it is the other way round - so 1234½ would be seen as

1.234,5. So the file could look like:
"Fish","1234"
"Meat","1235,5"
"Veg","1.236,6"
How do you import this data?
Answer:
Import using the Text Import wizard. When you get to Step 3 (column data format), there is a button called Advanced, which allows you to identify which is the thousands separator and which is the decimal point.

Notes: You can also do it by changing the regional settings of the computer control panel, regional information, then importing and then remembering to set it back, but this is more work and could have problems later if you forget to change it back.

Hour and Minute hands

116: In cell A1, you have a time, in the form hh:mm (for example 10:45). If you had a normal analog clock, the hour hand would be between the 10 and 11, and the minute hand would be on the 9. What formula can you put into cell B1 to show the angle between the clock hands?

Answer:
=ABS(MOD((MOD(A1,1)*720),360)-MOD((MOD(A1,1)*8640),360))

Notes: The hour hand goes round 2 times per day. Thus in 1 day, it covers 720°. The MOD 360 gives us the angle of the hour hand. The minute hand does 24 times per day, which is 24*360°, or 8640° and again MOD finds the angle. Subtracting finds the difference and ABS makes the angle a positive number (whichever hand is ahead of the other).This question requires some thinking, and it is very tempting to plough into a long formula that is huge when there is a much simpler solution.

Highlighting duplicates

117: You have a long column of values. Without sorting the values, how can you highlight any values that are duplicated? For example:

	A
1	Animal
2	Cat
3	Puma
4	Panther
5	Cheetah
6	Puma
7	Leopard

Answer:

Put in a conditional formula, with the condition being the following formula:

=COUNTIF($A$1:$A$7,A1)>1

And the format being a red background.

Notes: Often we are given a large table. We want to check for duplicates, but without making changes or adding formulae. This way allows us to spot duplication very quickly.

Snakes and Ladders

118: The numbers on a snakes and ladders board go backwards and forwards like this:

	A	B	C	D	E	F	G	H	I	J	K
1											
2		100	99	98	97	96	95	94	93	92	91
3		81	82	83	84	85	86	87	88	89	90
4		80	79	78	77	76	75	74	73	72	71
5		61	62	63	64	65	66	67	68	69	70
6		60	59	58	57	56	55	54	53	52	51
7		41	42	43	44	45	46	47	48	49	50
8		40	39	38	37	36	35	34	33	32	31
9		21	22	23	24	25	26	27	28	29	30
10		20	19	18	17	16	15	14	13	12	11
11		1	2	3	4	5	6	7	8	9	10

The formula which would be written in every cell and would generate these numbers was written as (formatted to make it easier

to read):
=IF(AND(OR(COLUMN()=2,ISODD(ROW())),
    OR(COLUMN()=11,ISEVEN(ROW()))),(11-ROW())*10+1,
    IF(ISODD(ROW()),J11+1,L11+1))

What is wrong with the formula and how should it be correctly written?

Answer:
The only error is that the AND and OR functions are swapped over. Thus the correct formula is:
=IF(OR(AND(COLUMN()=2,ISODD(ROW())),
    AND(COLUMN()=11,ISEVEN(ROW()))),(11-ROW())*10+1,
    IF(ISODD(ROW()),J11+1,L11+1))

Notes: Often you get long formulae, which may have been written by someone who either mis-typed it, did not know English as a first language, or just had a bad day. Finding errors in formulae and fixing them is crucial. Note that in some cells, the formula adds 1 to the cell to the left of it. Even though this would not happen in the left column, the formula has to refer to a potential column to the left. That's why the snakes and ladders board starts in column B. There is no need for it to start in row 2, but people often leave a space for aesthetic reasons.

Doing it by degrees

119: You have a column of your spreadsheet with temperatures typed in as numbers. However you want to show them as temperatures with ° F after them. How do you do this (including how you get the degree sign)?

	A
1	0° F
2	32° F
3	212° F

Answer:
Use a custom format to format the column as follows:
#° F
To get the degree sign in a format:

a) Press and keep your finger on the left ALT key
b) On the numeric keypad, type in 0, 1, 7 and 6
c) Release the ALT key.

Notes: The insert symbol does not work in a custom format, so you can't just insert symbol and then find the degree sign, you need to remember where it is. (You could have copied it and then pasted it in).

Deleting budget items

120: You have submitted your budget proposal in an Excel spreadsheet to your boss and he has used the drawing tool to put a red line through every item he wants removed. What is the easiest way of automatically removing these items?

Answer:

Unfortunately this is something that cannot be done. Theoretically, you could find the co-ordinates for each line, work out which cell (or cells) the line mostly crosses and then delete those entries, but the code would be horrific.

The only way to remove these items is to do it manually.

Notes: Not every problem is easily solved in Excel. There are times when you just have to do it manually, and an Excel programmer should be aware of what Excel can and can't do.

Zip codes

121: I have a spreadsheet of US names and addresses. In column H is their Zip code (a five-digit number). I want to ensure that whenever this row is entered, there is always 5 digits put in. What is the easiest way of doing this?

Answer:

a) Select the column
b) Select Data Validation from the Data ribbon
c) Under Allow, pick Text Length
d) Under Data, pick Equal to
e) Under Length, type in 5
f) Click OK.

This is shown below:

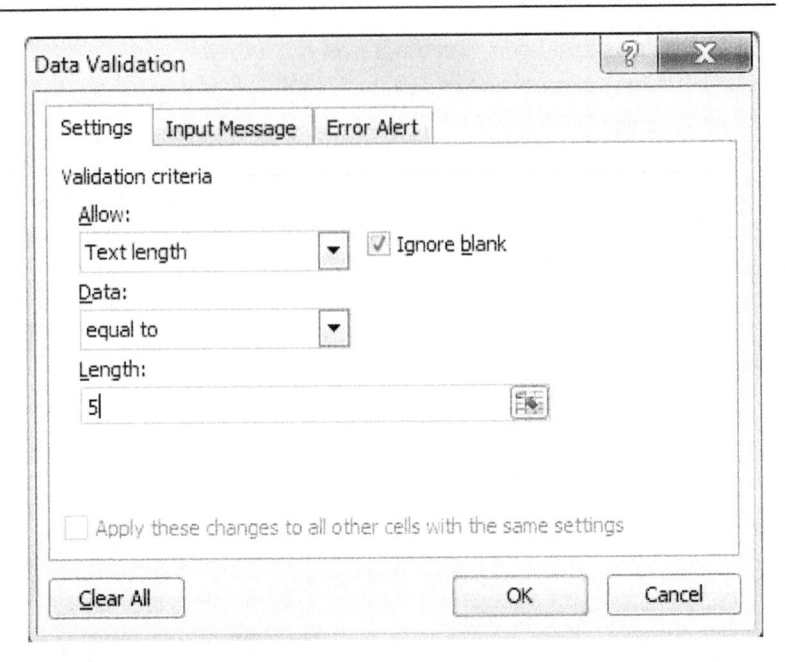

Notes: You can also add a pop-up when the cell is selected (to ask people to type in the five-digit zip code and/or an error message if they try and enter something too long or short.

Summing at top speed

122: You have numbers in the column from B2 to B9. You are in cell B10. What is the quickest way of putting a formula into cell B10 to sum the cells above (i.e. fewest key presses)?

Answer:
Press Alt = and Excel will type in the formula =sum(B2:B9) for you. Then press Enter.

Notes: A very quick way of using the most used function in Excel.

IP Addresses

123: IP (Internet protocol) addresses should be of the form 192.168.001.125. In other words there should be a full stop between each three digit set. How do I show this in an Excel cell (without converting the number to text)?

Answer:
Use the custom format of:

000\.000\.000\.000

Notes: Also useful for other specific formats, for example to show the price of something in Indian Rand, if it is 5 million rand, it would be shown as 5,00,000.

Best possible way

124: You have several options which can be adjusted, and need the values that give you the best result. What set of Excel functionality would you use for this and where would you find it?

Answer:
    a) You would use the Solver, or "what-if analysis tools".
    b) You would need to enable it through File -> Options -> Add-Ins -> Manage Excel Add-Ins:

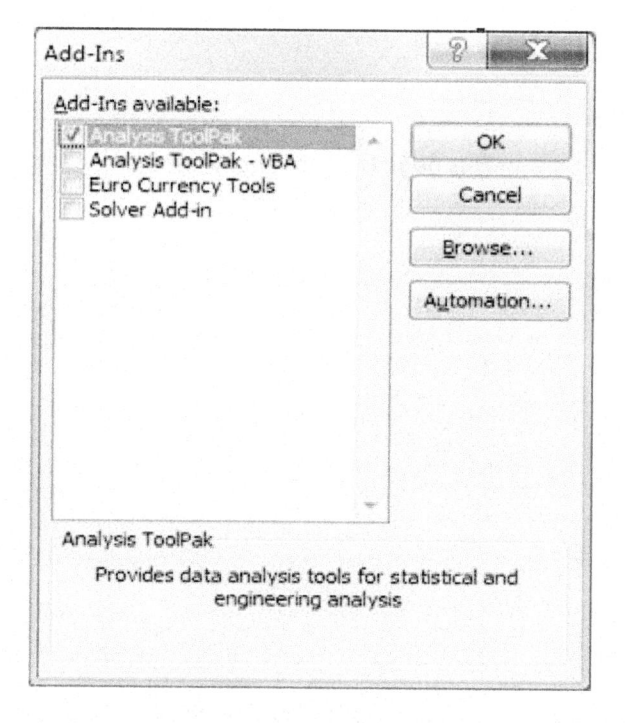

    c) Then enable the Solver Add-in and click OK.

Notes: If this is what you need, the solver is very powerful, but there is a learning curve.

This page is intentionally left blank

VBA / Coding

Hiding Sheets

125: One of the features of hiding a sheet is that another user can just come along and unhide it. How can you hide a sheet such that someone else can't just unhide it? What code would you use to apply this to Sheet1? If it is hidden such that they can't unhide it, can they still get the data from it?

Answer:

There is a property for sheets called xlSheetVeryHidden.

The code is:

ActiveWorkbook.Worksheets("sheet1").Visible = xlSheetVeryHidden

If it is hidden, anyone can get the data from it once they know what it is called. In this case using Sheet2, put in cell A1:

=Sheet1!A1

and dragging across and down.

Notes: This is a very useful feature for hiding sheets from people to prevent them editing the data and from messing up the spreadsheet (as most people don't know it even exists).Also, as identified, if you know the sheet name, you can still see the data, this is still not a problem because (1) they can't make changes to it, just see it and (2) if you make the sheet name something complex, e.g. SheetZYSTEJ34289, they are not going to guess it.

Automatic checking the syntax of your code

126: When writing VBA in Excel, how do you turn off the automatic syntax checking of your code?

Answer:

In the Options (Tools menu), in the Editor tab, untick the option "Auto Syntax Check":

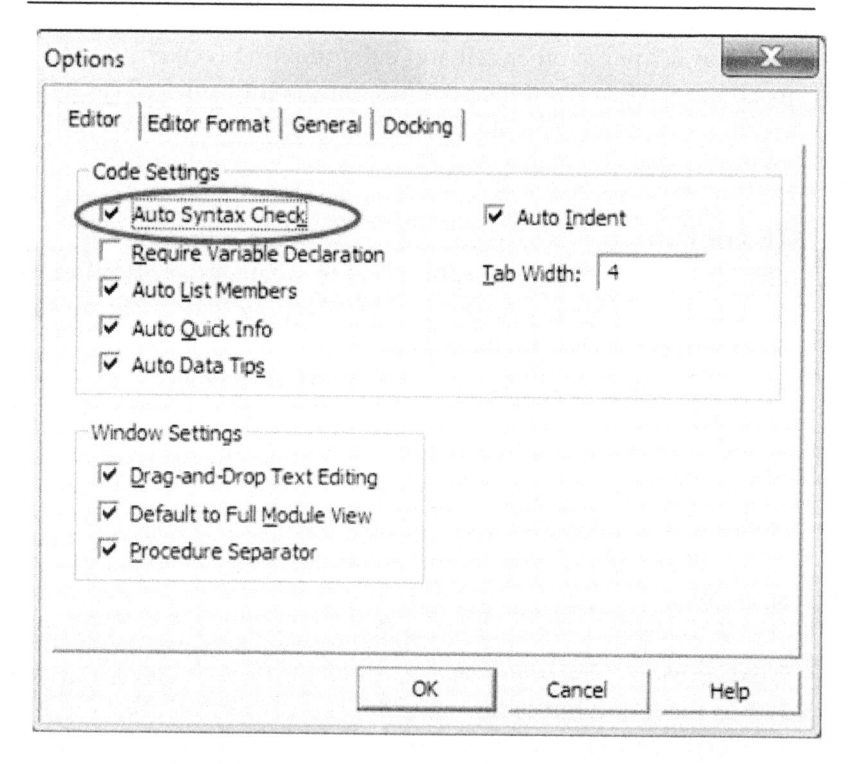

Advanced Excel Interview Questions You'll Most Likely Be Asked   77

Notes: Very useful if you are pasting code which then needs changing. You may not want syntax checking back on until you are ready.

Macro references
127: Is the default for macros to use relative, absolute or other references? Also, how do you change from one form to another?
Answer:
The default is to use absolute references. To change, select the Use Relative References in the Developer tab.

Notes: It can be very annoying, because you can record a macro and then run it from another cell and either nothing happens (because it just repeats when it did the previous time, in the same cells as it did it last time) or it can generate an error message which is often not clear why it means.

The ribbon

128: Often when you are using Excel to create an application, you want to turn off many of the Excel features so that users can focus on the functionality you have coded in.
What VBA code would you use to turn off the ribbon?
Answer:
Application.ExecuteExcel4Macro "SHOW.TOOLBAR(""Ribbon"",False)"
Notes: Not at all obvious, but a great boon in creating applications using Excel where you don't want the user to mess up your application.

Next, please

129: In the following code:
Sub SayThanks()
    Dim TheMessage As String
    TheMessage = "Thank you"
    Msgbox TheMessage
End Sub
If you are debugging the subroutine, which line will be highlighted when the user presses F8 once?
Answer:
TheMessage = "Thank you"
Notes: The yellow is the current line. It moves on to the next line of code, skipping declarations.

Understanding code 1

130: What does the following code do?
Private Sub Worksheet_Change(ByVal Target As Range)
   If Intersect(Target, Range("C5")) Is Nothing Then
     Exit Sub
   Else
    MsgBox "Remember to check the interest rates as well"

End If
End Sub
Answer:
Whenever cell C5 is changed, a message is displayed to check interest rates.

Notes: Understanding someone else's (often undocumented) code is a regular activity. Notice that the Exit Sub in this code doesn't do anything, but may have been put in because the ELSE part was originally very long and the writer wanted to make it clear that nothing else was going to happen if it hasn't changed.

My own macros

131: How do you store macros so that you can use them in any spreadsheet?
Answer:
When you create the macro, in the dialog box, under Store Macro In, select Personal Macro Workbook, as shown:

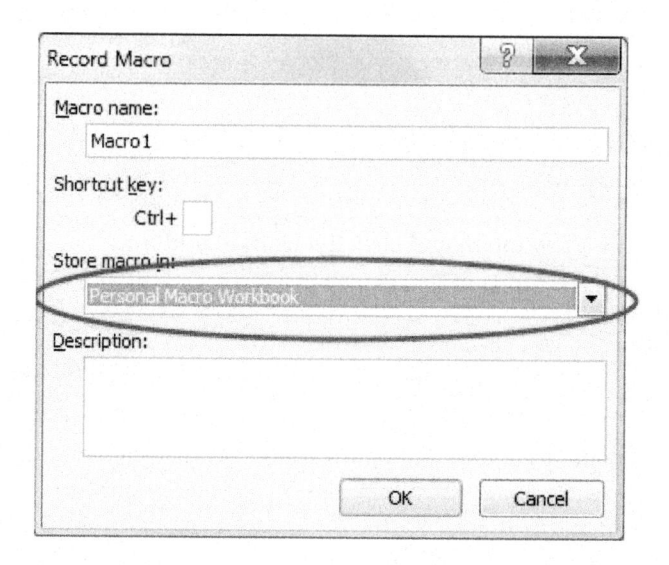

Notes: The default is to save it in this Workbook. However this lets you build up your own library of macros for functions you use regularly. This is very useful if, for example, you have a set of functions to run on every month's data.

1600 Pennsylvania avenue
132: In your VBA code, you want to check for cells content, but you don't mind if there are capital letters instead of lowercase (or vice versa). What code would you use to make the comparisons case insensitive?
Answer:
Option Compare Text
Notes: It has to appear at the top of a module.

Personal Workbooks
133: When you create a macro in the personal workbook, you can create it without a problem. You can also run it. However what happens (by default) when you try to edit it and how do you fix it?
Answer:
When you try and edit it, you will get the following message:

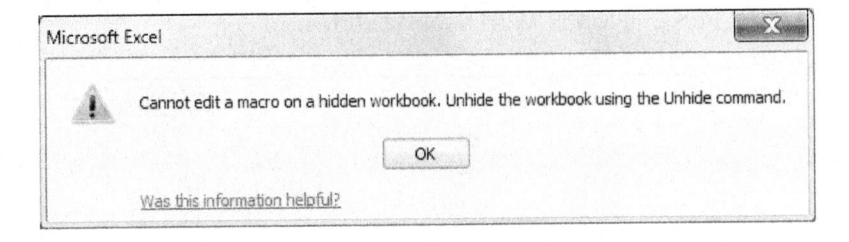

Go to the View menu and click the Unhide button:

Then ensure that your personal workbook is selected and click OK:

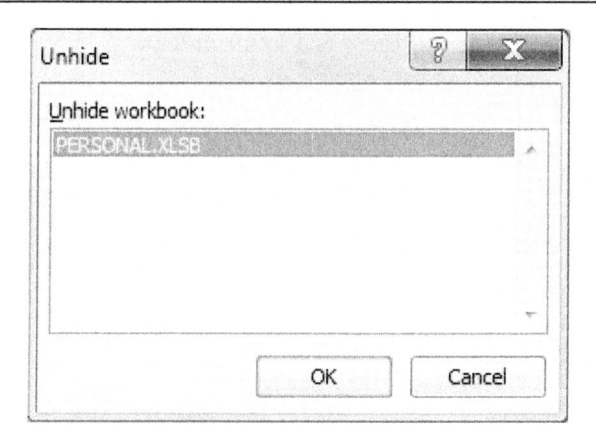

Now you can edit your personal macros.

Notes: It would be useful it the message at least told you where to find the Unhide command, but it doesn't.

VBA Tabs
134: In VBA, how do you change the number of spaces that are put in for each time TAB is pressed?
Answer:
Tools -> Options:

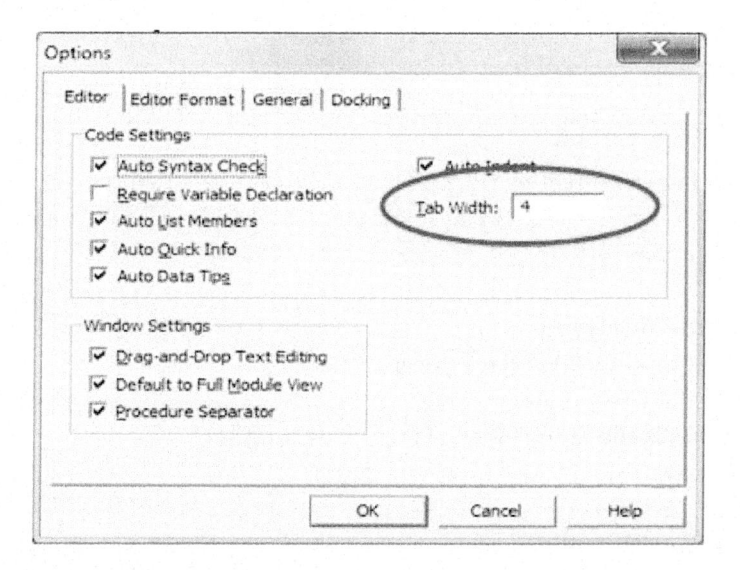

Notes: Useful if either there is a lot of indenting, or you are working on a narrow screen.

Function without comments

135: The following function has not been commented. What does it do?

Function CheckText(Haystack As String, Needle As String) As Boolean
    CheckText = " " & UCase(Haystack) & " " Like "*[!A-Z]" & UCase(Needle) & "[!A-Z]*"
End Function

Answer:

The Find function allows you to find a set of characters in a cell, for example to find "jumps" in "the quick brown fox jumps over the lazy dog". However what if you are searching for a word and don't want your formula to pick it up in another word. For example "pen" in "the pen is mighty" will be found but it will not trigger in "metalwork and carpentry". You can't guarantee that there are spaces round it as there may be punctuation marks around.

This function finds if the "Word" is in the "text" as a word.

For example, in the following sheet, the cell C1 has the formula.

= CheckText(A1,B1)

	A	B	C
1	The pencil and pen.	Pen	TRUE

Notes: With real-world problems such as this, often the variables, in this case Needle and Haystack, give you a hint. Also the name of the function can help.

Little numbers

136: In my VBA, I have the code:
Dim LittleNumber as Byte
What is the range of values for LittleNumber?
Answer:
0 to 255

Notes: This is one of the easiest, and thus exact values should be known.

Excel window size
137: In VBA, how do you find the dimensions of the current Excel window?
Answer:
appWidth = Application.Width
appHeight = Application.Height
Anything can be on the left of the equals signs.
Notes: Generally used to ensure that everything fits on the screen.

File already in existence?
138: In VBA, how do you check if the file c:\output.txt already exists?
Answer:
FileExists = dir("c:\output.txt")
If FileExists is empty ("") then file does not exist, otherwise it does.

Msgbox
139: You are writing VBA which will ask a question:
MsgBox "Do you want to continue?",
You want there to be a question mark symbol, an OK button and a Cancel button. How should the line of code end?
Answer:
MsgBox "Do you want to continue?",vbOkCancel+vbQuestion
OR
MsgBox "Do you want to continue?", vbQuestion+vbOkCancel
Notes: The message box is a popular command and it should be used correctly.

Delays
140: You want your code to delay for 30 minutes before starting (because you have triggered other code which may take up to 30 minutes to generate the data that Excel will be importing). What VBA instruction(s) would you use to generate the 30 minute delay?
Answer:
Application.Wait (Now + TimeValue("0:30:00"))
Notes: You could split it up into multiple instructions (creating a variable, then running the application.wait) Note that

application.wait is not very accurate and could be up to a second out. So it's fine for 30 minutes, but if the answer of:
Application.Wait (Now + TimeValue("0:30:01"))
were given (i.e. 30 minutes + a second or two more) that would be fine.

Selection
141: What does the following code do?
ActiveCell.Resize(1,4).Select
Answer:
It selects the current cell and the three to the right of it.
Notes: Used in VBA to select a relative area.

Running a macro
142: I have an Excel worksheet with a macro. How do I create a button that runs that macro?
Answer:
a) Firstly you need to turn on the Developer tab (it is OFF by default). This is done by: File -> Options -> Customize ribbon and tick the Developer toolbar and click OK.
b) Go to the developer toolbar and select Insert -> Form -> Button
c) Then select the macro from the list of macros in this spreadsheet and click OK.

Notes: The above way of showing the Developer toolbar is correct in the current version of Excel (2010).In Excel 2003, showing the Developer toolbar was done by: File -> Excel Options -> Popular -> Show Developer tab in the ribbon

Understanding code 2
143: What does the following code do?
Sub ProcessPrices()
  Dim i As Integer
  For i = 1 to 200
    If Range("A" & CStr(i)).Value > Range("B" & CStr(i)).Value Then
      Range("B" & CStr(i)).Value = Range("A" & CStr(i)).Value
    End If

Next
msgBox "Processing complete."
End Sub
Answer:
It goes down column A and if the value next to each cell (in column B) is lower, it replaces it with the higher value.
From the name of the sub, the expectation is that it is working on prices.
Notes: Used for using the highest (or lowest) prices, or the most recent dates.

Disabling macros
144: One computer has all macros enabled. As this could be a security risk (because a macro could do anything), you want to turn this back to the default where macros are normally disabled but with the user notified. How do you do this?
Answer:
File -> Options -> Trust center -> Trust Center Settings -> Macro settings
The options there are now clear.
Notes: This is very well hidden.

Binding
145: What is the preferred method of binding? Which method of binding is fastest?
Answer:
Microsoft recommends early binding in almost all cases. In terms of overall execution speed, it is at least twice as fast as late binding.

Counting characters
146: I have text in cells from A2 to A22. What formula do I need to calculate the total number of characters in these cells?
Answer:
Either
=sum(len(A2:A22))
and press Control-Shift-Enter, OR
{=sum(len(A2:A22))}
which is how the formula will show on the screen.

Notes: This is an example of the usage of an array formula.

Saving Macros
147: I start to record a macro and ask for it to be stored in my Personal Marco Workbook:

What is the filename of the file that will hold my macro?
Answer:
Personal.xlsb

Timing
148: When does the following code run?
Private Sub MyForm_Initialize()
   MsgBox "Initialize"
End Sub
Answer:
When the form is loaded
Notes: It is important to know when events are run.

Variable Requisition
149: In the options below:

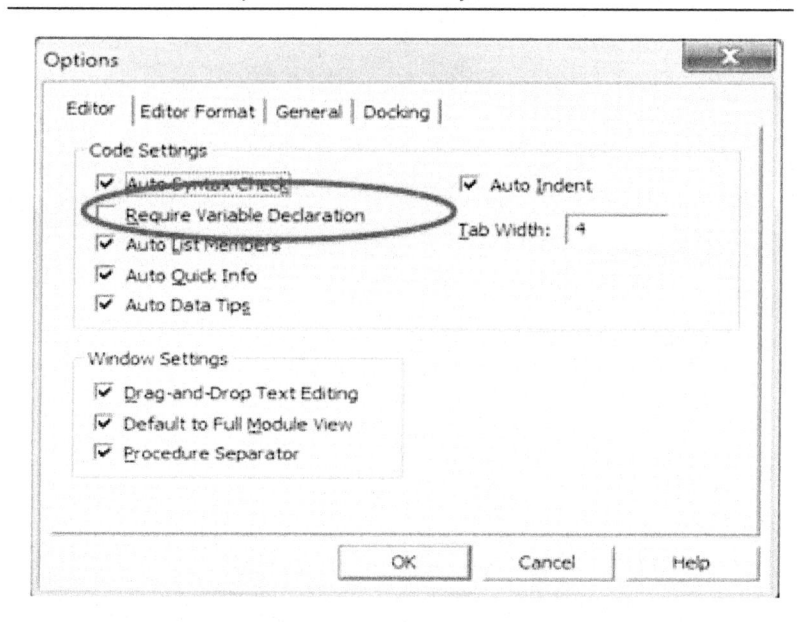

if Require Variable Declaration is ticked, what words will be put at the start of any new module?
Answer:
Option Explicit
Notes: The "Require Variable Declaration" gives you the "option explicit" and the "Option Explicit" is the bit that requires variables to be declared. So you can put in "Option Explicit" on your own (to ensure your variables are declared), or remove it manually.

This page is intentionally left blank

Specific Uses

Testing the specific uses of Excel, for example as a database, financial or statistical analysis tool

Data Analysis

150: You have a column of numbers and want to do a variety of basis analysis to understand what data you have, such as sum, mean, minimum and standard deviation. What alternative is there to typing in a separate formula for each one?

Answer:

There is a function called Descriptive Analysis which gives you (in one go) the whole lot, for example:

Data	Column1	
1		
2	Mean	14.41667
6	Standard Error	7.362331
5	Median	5.5
6	Mode	6
43	Standard Deviation	25.50386
8	Sample Variance	650.447
6	Kurtosis	6.602375
87	Skewness	2.590974
2	Range	86
3	Minimum	1
4	Maximum	87
	Sum	173
	Count	12

A longer answer may explain that this is part of the data analysis toolpack.

Notes: The data analysis toolpack is not installed by default (probably because it takes up memory and few people use it), but provides a range of functions (mostly statistical such as regression). However simple data analysis can help with a first view on the set of data that you have.

Repayments on a loan

151: You want to work out the monthly repayments on a loan of $1000, borrowed for 5 years at 5% APR, as shown below (all numbers were entered as numbers and then reformatted as shown below).

	A	B
1	Amount	$ 1,000.00
2	Years	5
3	APR	5%

What formula would you write to calculate how much each repayment is?
Answer:
One thing to notice is that you are required to work out monthly repayments, but are given the loan term in years. You need to multiply the number of years by 12 to get months. You also need to divide the APR by 12 to get the monthly interest rate. So the formula is:
=PMT(C4/12,C3*12,C2)
Notes: This tests both the knowledge of the PMT function (without specifically mentioning it) as well as the ability to work out what changes to make when converting from years to months.

Fractions
152: In the spreadsheet below, the value in column B is one sixth of the value of column A. What is the simplest way of generating the fractions as shown below?

	A	B
1	1	1/6
2	2	1/3
3	3	1/2
4	4	2/3
5	5	5/6
6	6	1

Answer:
In B1, put in the formula:
=A1/6
And drag down to B6. Then select the fractions format from the list of

formats.
Notes: Obviously this could be done by a long formula, but the question did ask for the easiest method.

School Timetable

153: I am using Excel to prepare a school timetable. I have one sheet named for each of "Geography", "History", "General Science", "Religious-Education", "English", "PE" and so on. What is the problem?
Answer:
You cannot use the word "History" as the name of a tab.
Notes: "General Science" is ok as you can have a space in the name of a sheet. A hyphen is also ok. Also "PE" is not too short, or "Religious-Education" too long.

Protection

154: What is the difference between workbook and worksheet protection?
Answer:
Workbook protection asks for a password to open the workbook (or to make changes). You are always asked for a password.
Worksheet protection prevents you from making some changes (specified when the protection is applied). You are only asked for a password if you want to unlock the worksheet (for example to perform one of those prevented changes).
Notes: There is also VB protection.

Tax calculations

155: I need to calculate tax. The way the tax works is as follows: if the person earns up to $5,000, they pay 10% tax. If they earn between $5,000 and $50,000, they pay 10% on the first $5,000 and then 20% on the rest. And if they earn over $50,000, they pay 10% on the first $5,000, 20% on the bit up to $50,000 and then 25% on the rest. So my initial spreadsheet looks like this (all numbers entered as numbers and then formatted):

	A	B	C
1	From	To	Tax
2	$0	$5,000	10%
3	$5,000	$50,000	20%
4	$50,000		25%
5			
6	Amount Earned	Tax to pay	
7	$50,000	$9,750	

As any of the numbers may change, they should all be referred to by cell. Fortunately any changes will not change the number of rates (from three).

What formula should be in cell B7?

Answer:

=IF(A7<B2,A7*C2,B2*C2+IF(A7<B3,(A7-A3)*C3,(B3-A3)*C3+(A7-A4)*C4))

Dollar signs in front of any of the number or letter parts of the cells are also fine, for example A7 could be shown as A7, $A7, A$7 or $A$7.

Notes:

The formula breaks down into:

= IF(A7<B2,	Is the earnings less than the $5,000
A7*C2,	If so, all that needs to be paid is the earnings times 10%
B2*C2+	If not, they at least need to pay the $5,000 times 10%
IF(A7<B3,	Is the earnings less than the $50,000
(A7-A3)*C3,	If so add the difference between their pay and $5000 times 20%
(B3-A3)*C3+	If not, they need to pay the $50,000 times 20% . . .
(A7-A4)*C4))	plus the remainder at 25%

Sorting Data

156: In the following spreadsheet, the products have been laid out horizontally.

	A	B	C
1	Wood	Stone	Concrete
2	Windows	Doors	Walls
3	Kitchen	Lounge	Bathroom
4	Paint	Tiles	Wallpaper
5	Radiators	Lights	Fireplaces
6	Sockets	Conduit	Cables
7	Pipes	Faucets	Waste

We want them so that they are all in one column, with the first row initially and then the next and so on, i.e.

	A
1	Wood
2	Stone
3	Concrete
4	Windows
5	Doors
6	Walls
7	Kitchen

and so on. We have allocated sheet2 for this sorted data. What formula do we put into Sheet2!A1 to drag down and sort all the data for us (i.e. without changing the source data)?

Answer:

=OFFSET(Sheet1!$A$1,INT((ROW()-1)/3),MOD((ROW()-1),3))

Notes: Here is an example where a "real-life" problem has been presented and what is wanted is known, but no indication as to how to achieve it. The student is left to figure out what formula would perform the action.

Membership List

157: The membership list for my association looks like this:

	A	B	C
1	Mrs Emily White		
2	Reverend John Green		
3	Doctor Arvind Black		

(all the other data appears in columns after D).
Luckily, all the data in column A has been entered in the format of title, first name and lastname (as shown). I will want to do sorting on last name, and some mail merging, so I want each of these in separate columns. This is the titles in column A, the firstnames in column B and the lastnames in column C. What is the easiest way of doing this?

Answer:
a) Select column A
b) In the Data Ribbon select Text to Columns.
c) Select Delimited and Next.
d) Tick the box next to "Space" and click Finish.

Notes: The point here is to realise there is functionality in Excel to do this for you and you don't have to write formulae if they are not needed.

Headers

158: What VBA is needed to specify a header on the current Excel worksheet as the following?
Font: Times New Roman
Size: 12 points
Style: Bold
Alignment: Centered
Text: June

Answer:
ActiveSheet.PageSetup.CenterHeader = "&""Times New Roman,Bold""&12June"

Statistical analyses

159: You have written a spreadsheet in Microsoft Excel 2010 using statistical functions that were all available in Excel 2003. However when you ship it to your colleague in Microsoft Excel 2003, he complains that some of his results are different from yours. Give two possible causes.

Answer:
a) If your spreadsheet used random numbers (or numbers based on the current time, etc) then the numbers would be different and thus any calculations based on them would be

different.

b) The accuracy of various statistical functions has been improved from Excel 2003 to 2010. Thus the answers you get will be more accurate than his. In some cases there can be a large difference.

Notes: There are often many, very different reasons why something can happen. The first answer is not always the right one.

Time to pay off loan

160: How long will it take to pay off a $12,000 loan at $400 per month, with interest at 0.5% per month?

	A	B
1	Loan	$12,000
2	Monthly Payments	400
3	Interest Rate per month	0.5%
4	How many installments to pay off	

What formula should I put into cell B4?
Answer:
=NPER(B3,-B2,B1)
Also acceptable is:
=CEILING(NPER(B3,-B2,B1),1)
To round up as you will need to make that last payment (even though the amount will be less than $400.
Notes: B3 and –B2 are correct as interest rate and repayments are both monthly.
It is –B2 because we are reducing the loan.
The answer will be in number of months.

Recording Macros

161: Where is the icon - or where are the icons - which allow you to start recording a macro?
Answer:
One is on the developer's ribbon (which will need turning ON via File -> Options -> Ribbons), and the other is on the bottom left of the

screen.

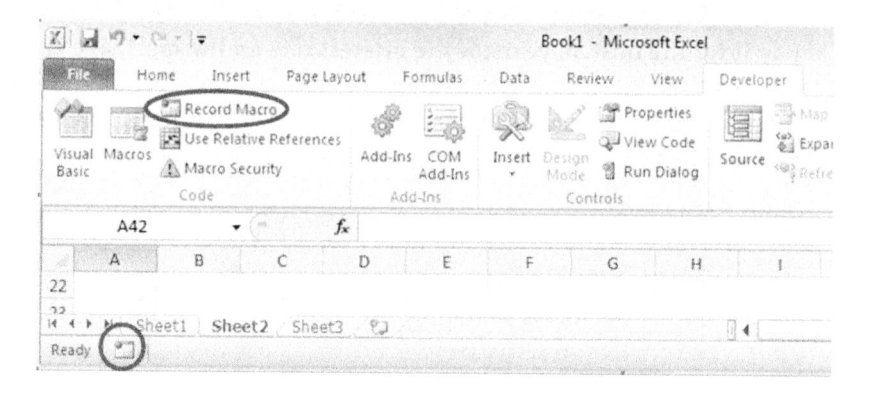

Notes: This is an example of Excel offering the same functionality in more than one place. Although it might make it easier to find, it does increase the clutter on the screen.

Macro starting
162: How do you get a macro to automatically run as soon as Excel loads the workbook?
Answer:
Call the macro Auto_Open.
Notes: Useful if, for example, there are dates or similar information which could be updated when the spreadsheet opens. Also for importing a current file at the start (such as output from another program).

Macro not starting
163: You have a macro that runs automatically when Excel loads the workbook. How do you stop it from running as a one-off or for the future?
Answer:
   a) Press the Shift key when you open the spreadsheet.
   b) Rename the macro.
Notes: Some macros load some data, perform some calculations, save the data and then quit. You need to bypass the auto_open macro to make any changes to the spreadsheet.

Buying houses

164: I can afford to pay $1,000 per month for a house, and I expect to pay it for the next 30 years. If the interest rate on the mortgage is 5% per year, I want to find what value of a house I can afford. Ignoring other numbers such as insurance and taxes, what formula should I put into B4?

	A	B
1	Monthly Payments	1000
2	Mortgage rate per year	5%
3	Duration (years)	30
4	House Value	

Answer:
=PV(B2/12,B3*12,-B1).
Notes: B2/12 because the rate is per year and the payments are monthly.
B3*12 because the duration is in months and again payments are monthly.
-B1 because I am paying off the amount each month.
The actual answer is $186,281.62.

Feature List

165: You want to list the features of two products, like this:

	A	B	C
1	Product	Screw	Nail
2	Twisty bit	✓	✗
3	Smooth edges	✗	✓
4	Pointy end	✓	✓

How do you put the ticks and crosses in?
Answer:
Use the Symbol option on the Insert ribbon and then select the font and symbols you want.

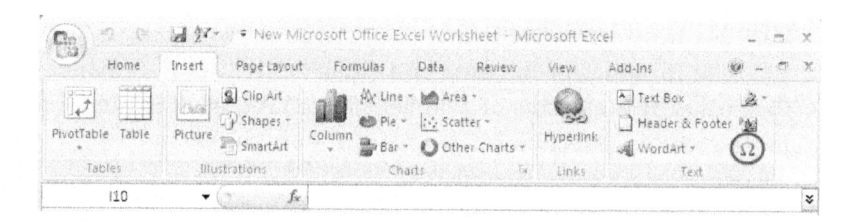

The ticks and crosses above come from the Windings font, but there are other fonts also offering ticks and crosses.

Notes: If you ship this spreadsheet to someone else, they may not have the same fonts, so if you are planning to ship it, it is better to use common fonts such as Wingdings or to export the file to PDF.

Dice game

166: In our local dice game, we need to roll four dice and then add up the highest three. I have created an Excel spreadsheet.

	A	B
1	First die	
2	Second die	
3	Third die	
4	Fourth dice	
5	Sum of highest 3	

What formula would I need for cell B1 to get a random number from 1 to 6 (so that I can drag it down to B2:B4)?

What is the simplest formula for B5 to add up the highest of the dice in the cells above?

Answer:
The formula for cells B1 (to B4) is:
=RANDBETWEEN(1,6)
And the simplest formula for B5 is
=SUM(B1:B4)-MIN(B1:B4)

Notes: You could use rand() to generate a number from 0 to 1 and then extend the range and round, but randbetween() does it all for you. The second formula is much easier. Instead of trying to figure out which are the highest three, just add up the lot and then deduct the lowest one.

Going round in Circles

167: The formula for the area of a circle is: $Area = \pi r^2$, where r is the radius. If the radius of a circle is in cell A1, what is the formula for the area of that circle?

Answer:

=PI()*A1^2

OR

=PI()*A1*A1

Notes: This tests the * for multiply and the PI function, which is more accurate than, say $\frac{22}{7}$.

Graphs, Drawing and Pictures

Polar Charts

168: What is a polar chart and when would you use it?
Answer:
It is a graphical chart showing multivariate data. It shows 3 or more points where the values cannot be directly compared to each other, like reliability, speed and comfort in the example below.

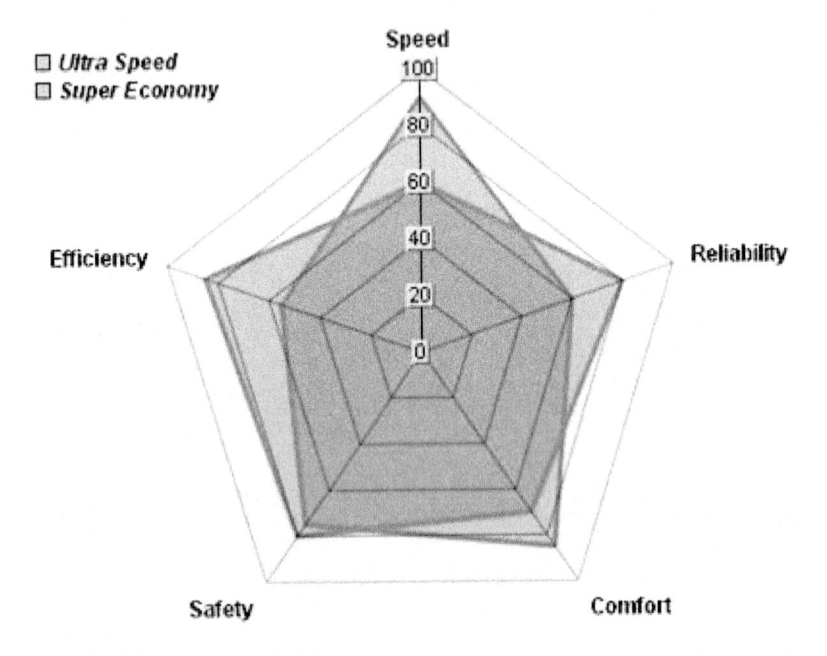

Each "spoke" is equally spaced and there is usually the same scale for all spokes.

Reducing file size

169: When saving your spreadsheet, it is huge. You have not that much data or formulae in, so it must be down to those high quality pictures you put in and then shrunk. As this spreadsheet will only be printed on a standard laser printer, how can you reduce the resolution of the graphics so that the file size is reduced?
Answer:
Under the File menu, Save As, there is a small "Tools" option and under it there is an option "Compress Pictures" which will do this for you.

Advanced Excel Interview Questions You'll Most Likely Be Asked   103

Notes: Also useful when sending spreadsheets by email.

Putting a chart onto a new sheet
170: You have a chart on the current worksheet. However now you want to move it so that it is on a sheet of its own. How do you do this?
Answer:
Click on the graph and then use the move chart option on the Design ribbon as shown below:

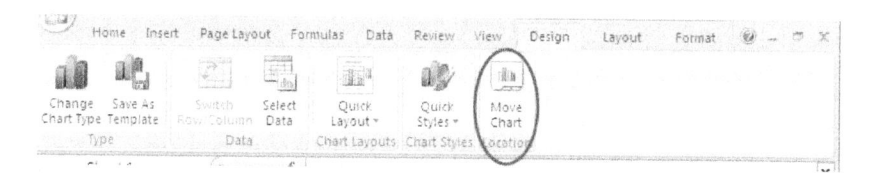

Notes: Not obvious where to find it, as it's not with any other similar commands. However useful once found.

Editing pictures
171: I have a picture in my spreadsheet (the picture on the left) and I want to blur the edges (to get the picture on the right). Which of the Microsoft Office / Windows programs should I transfer it into to blur the edges and how do I do it?

Answer:
Excel will do this for you. Just click on the picture (which will give you a format tab) and then select the style with the blurred edges.
Notes: Some functionality that previously was the control of specialized art packages is now included in Excel.

Putting loops around data

172: Our sales report over the years 2009-2011 looks like this:

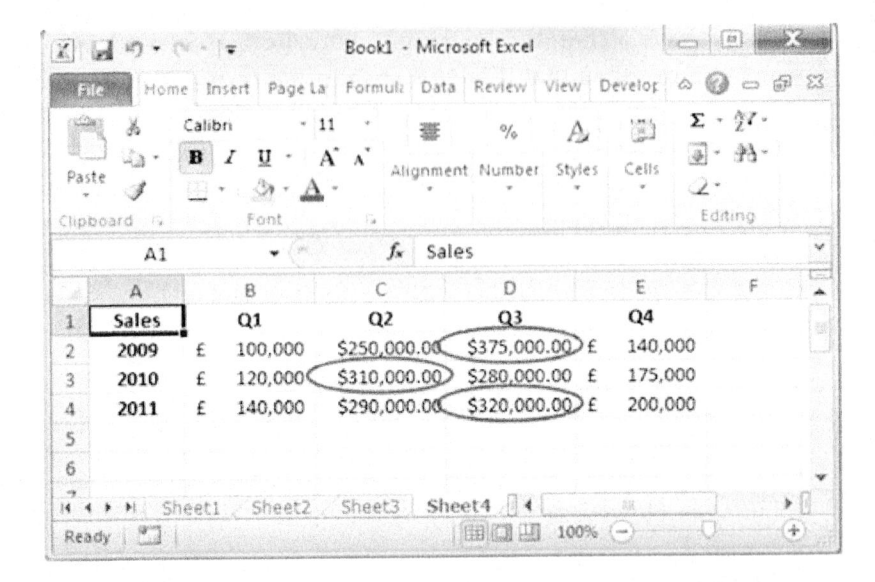

	A	B	C	D	E
1	Sales	Q1	Q2	Q3	Q4
2	2009	£ 100,000	$250,000.00	$375,000.00 £	140,000
3	2010	£ 120,000	$310,000.00	$280,000.00 £	175,000
4	2011	£ 140,000	$290,000.00	$320,000.00 £	200,000

We want to circle all quarters where sales were over $300,000 (as shown). How can we get Excel to do this without having to do each one manually?

Answer:
   a) Select the turnover numbers (in this case B2:D4)
   b) In the Data ribbon, open Data Validation window
   c) Set the fields to: Whole number, less than and 300000 and click OK
   d) In the Data Validation dropdown, select Circle Invalid Data

Notes: In this case, we are using the marking of data as "invalid data" to enable the ability of Excel to put circles round them. It is one of the advantages (and disadvantages) of Excel to be able to use the tools provided for a range of uses, not just the ones they are normally meant for.

Gandtt Charts

173: I have a spreadsheet as below and want to add a Gandtt chart (as shown). How do I create the floating brown bars?

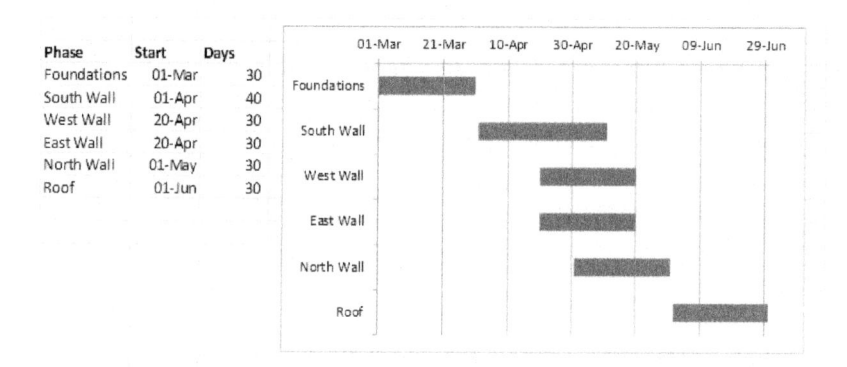

Phase	Start	Days
Foundations	01-Mar	30
South Wall	01-Apr	40
West Wall	20-Apr	30
East Wall	20-Apr	30
North Wall	01-May	30
Roof	01-Jun	30

Answer:
You create a bar chart of the data (which will look like this). You may need to adjust the X axis.

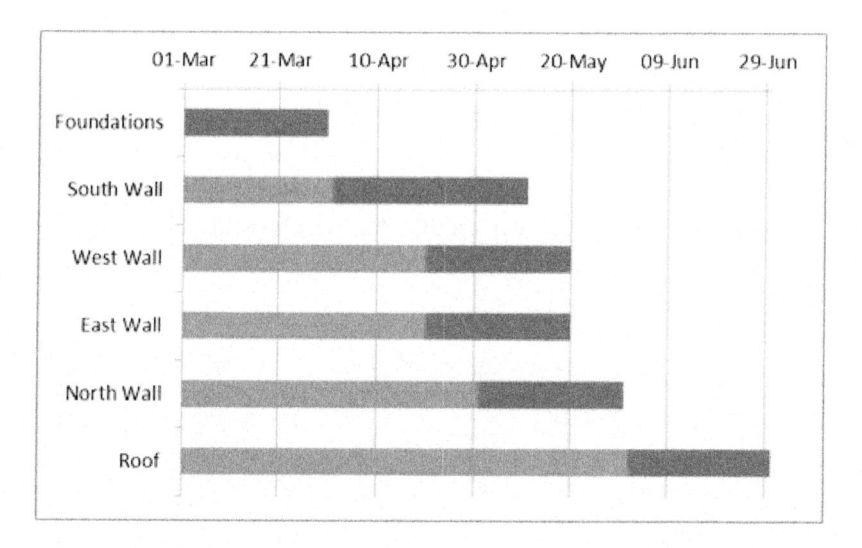

Then you just format the blue bars as "No fill" and you get the floating brown bars.

Notes: Again using the features built into Excel to address a real-world problem.

Doughnuts
174: What types of data values cannot be shown on a Doughnut graph?

Answer:
Negative values. Also values of 0 are not visible, but can be labeled.
Notes: Doughnut graphs are not used much, for a range of reasons. One of which is that they cannot show negative numbers.

Drawing Circles

175: I want to draw a circle on my spreadsheet using shapes. How do I do this?
Answer:
Excel does not have a circle per se, but does have an "oval" (which is actually an ellipse). If you select this, mark the top left and then put your finger on the Shift key, which will restrain the shape to a circle. When you release the mouse button, you will have a circle.
Notes: Usage of the shift key to restrict the shape being drawn is a useful function. It also restricts rectangles to squares, arrows to 45° and so on.

Multiple colors in graphs

176: I have a graph of 4 points, where (as you would expect) all the points show up in the same color. What is the easiest way of making each of them a different color - as shown below?

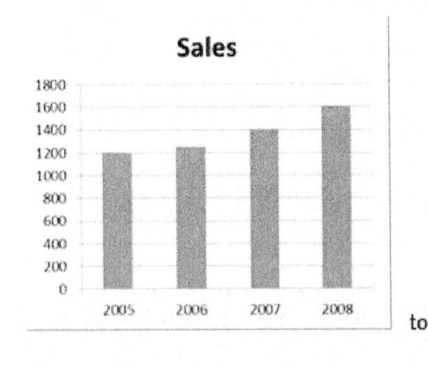

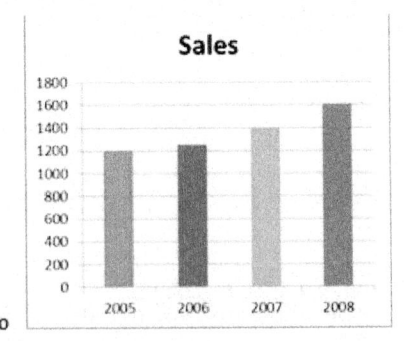

Answer:
The easiest way is to right click on any bar and select Format Data Series -> Fill -> Vary colors by point.
Notes: Nice feature, quick and easy to implement - once you know about it.

Instant graphs

177: You have a spreadsheet such as the one below. What is the quickest way of graphing the data (i.e. to produce the graph shown)?

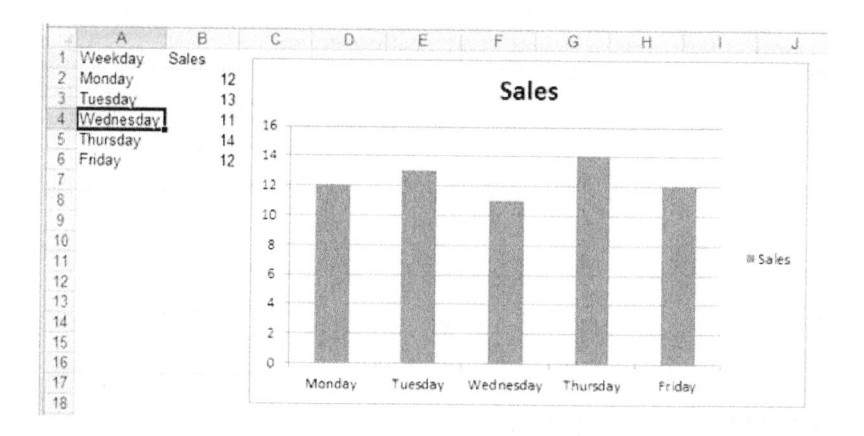

Answer:
The quickest way is to just press Alt-F1. Excel finds the area and the titles and produces the whole graph instantly.

Notes: A very quick way of spotting unusual data (such as one entry a thousand times the others) and getting a feel for the data and the general trend.

Loading a picture

178: I have a worksheet which shows the personal details of a person. One of the details is in cell B4 – it is the filename of their picture, all files being stored in the directory c:\pictures. I have an image (called image1) for the picture to be shown in. What VBA code do I need to do to put their picture onto the screen?

Answer:
Me.Image1.Picture = LoadPicture("c:\pictures\" & range("B4"))

Notes: Note the \ after the pictures so that the path is complete.

Pictures not printing in color

179: My pictures on my spreadsheet are not printing in color. What Excel setting might I have done to cause this and how can I turn it off?

Answer:

There is an option that reduces everything to black and white. If the rest of the spreadsheet is in black and white, the lack of color elsewhere may not have been noticed. It can be set from Page Setup (Page Layout ribbon or File -> Print) and in the Sheet tab there is an option for printing in just Black and White.

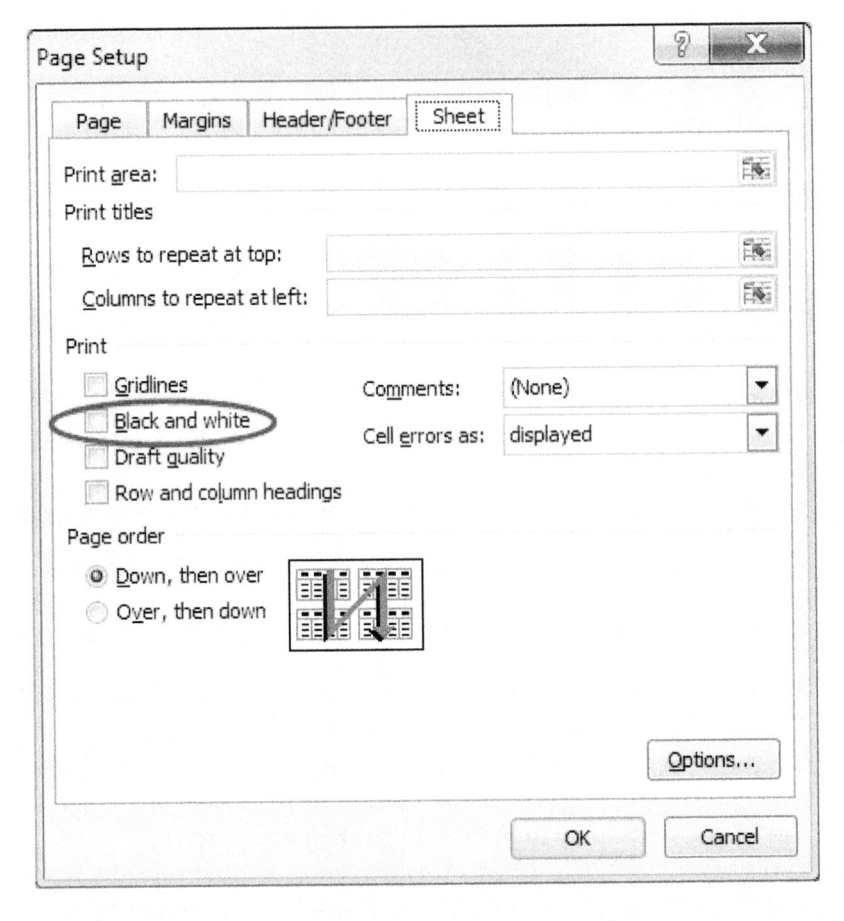

Notes: In these cases it is worth checking if text prints in color and if other applications can print in color as it may be a printer setting. In this case the question specifically asked for an Excel setting.

Drop Lines
180: What are Drop lines and how are they added to a graph?

Answer:
Drop lines are simply lines in some types of charts that go vertically from the data point down (or up) to the horizontal axis. They help you to determine the X value (for example, the date) where each data point occurs.

You can add them via the Lines option on the layout toolbar:

Notes: Excel offers Drop lines for Line charts and Area charts; the option is disabled for other chart types.

Border control
181: You have selected an area of cells. What is the shortcut key to:
    a) Add a border round the cells?
    b) Remove the border round the cells?
    c) Open Format cells dialog box to apply specific borders?

Answer:
    a) To apply an outside border, press Control Shift &
    b) To remove the outside border, press Control Shift _
    c) To open Format cells, press Control 1

Notes: Some people mainly use Excel to produce tables, so these shortcuts can help make things much quicker.

Trend Lines
182: What types of trend lines does Microsoft Excel support directly (i.e. without having to write them yourself)?

Answer:
    a) Exponential
    b) Linear
    c) Logarithmic
    d) Polynomial
    a) e). Power
    b) f.) Moving Average

Notes: In the Format Trendline dialog box available from right clicking a graph line:

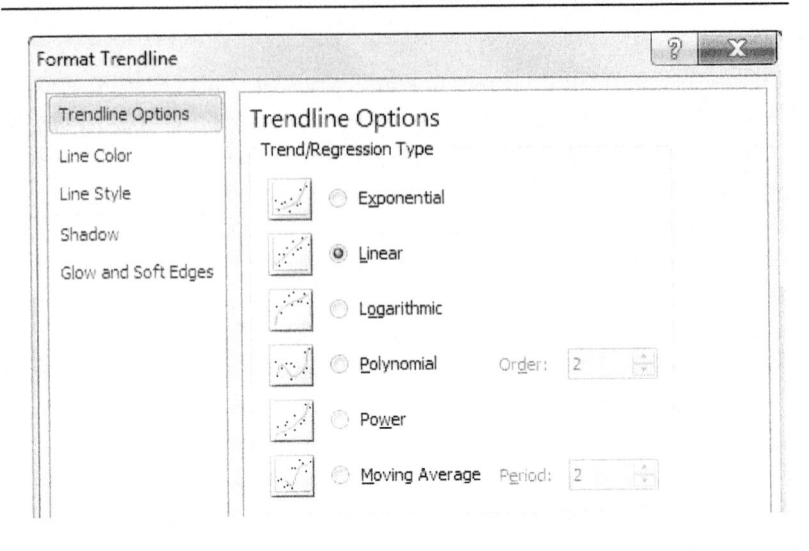

Thousands

183: I have a graph showing sales for each employee:

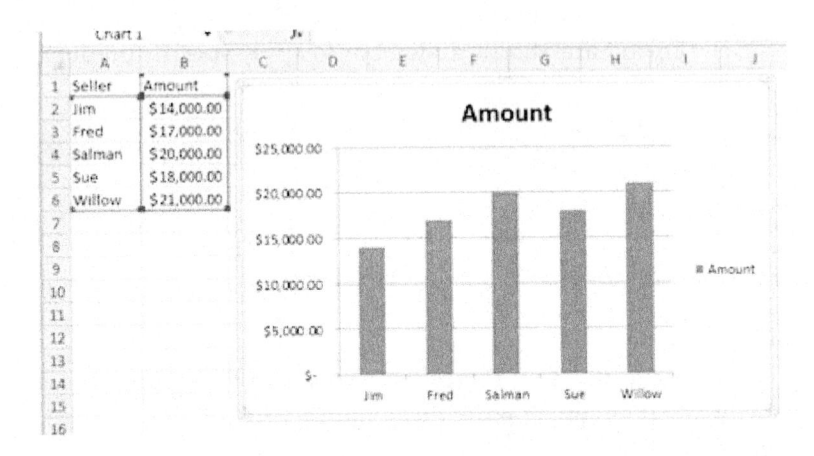

I want to simplify the graph to just show the number of thousands of dollars (rather than the full amount including cents). How can I easily do this?

Answer:
In the Layout ribbon, select Axes -> Primary Vertical Axis -> Show Axis in thousands.

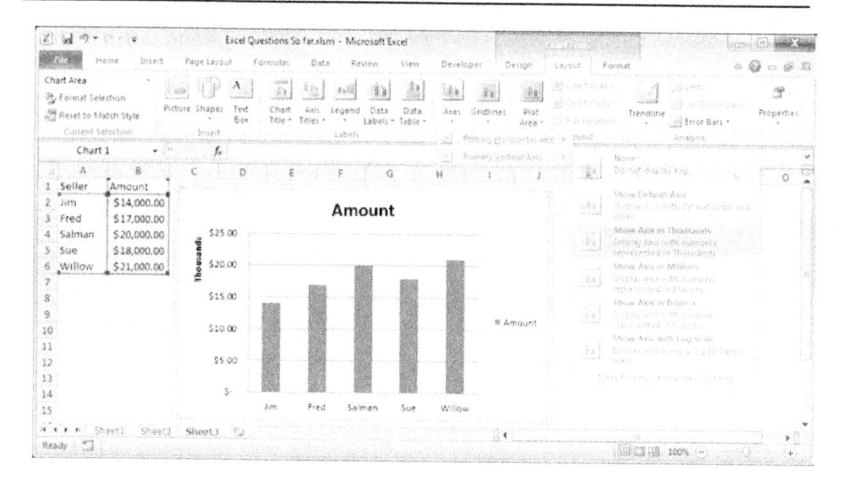

Advanced Excel Interview Questions You'll Most Likely Be Asked 111

[Screenshot of Excel showing a bar chart titled "Amount" with data: Jim $14,000.00, Fred $17,000.00, Salman $20,000.00, Sue $18,000.00, Willow $21,000.00]

Notes: Quick and easy. Note that the label on the Y axis also changes to show the word "Thousands".

Drawing attention to points in sparklines
184: In sparklines, which points can you ask to be shown to draw attention to them (e.g. the highest?)
Answer:
    a) The highest
    b) The lowest
    c) The first point
    d) The last point
    e) Any negative points
    f) All points (markers)

Notes: These are useful to get a feel of the data.

Moving the captions for the graph
185: You have a graph with multiple lines, but would prefer the key to be below the graph instead of to the right. What is the easiest way of moving them?

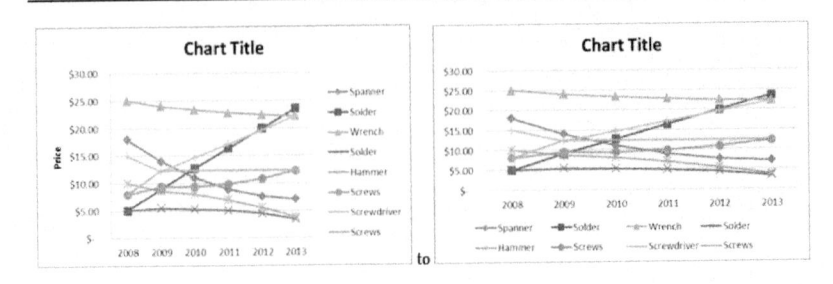

Answer:
Use the Chart Layout option on the Design tab.

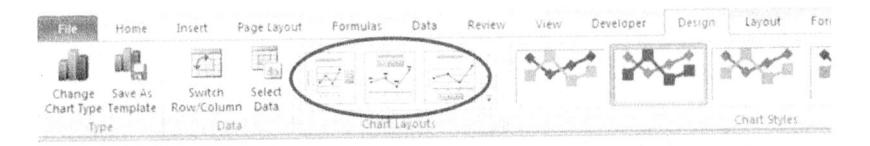

Notes: They are usually better on the right if you have a low number of points on the X axis, or below if you have a lot of points. Also there are many layouts which you can get quick and easy. Access the rest from the dropdown on the bottom right of the three layouts shown.

Counting down
186: If each column represents a year earlier than the previous (rather than the next year which is more common), how can you get the sparklines to show the data with time going forwards?
Answer:
   a) Click on the sparklines
   b) Go to the Design ribbon
   c) Go to the Axis menu and select Plot Data Right to Left as shown below:

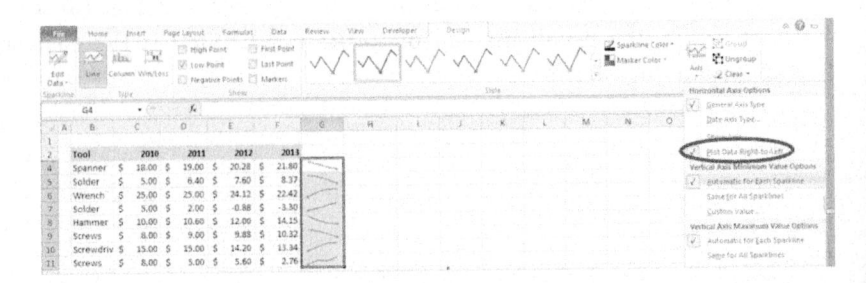

Shade area in-between
187:

	A	B	C
1	Date	Low	High
2	Mar 1	12	20
3	Mar 2	15	23
4	Mar 3	14	18
5	Mar 4	17	19
6	Mar 5	15	20
7	Mar 6	16	18

I want a graph, showing the horizontal gridlines, but only the area between the two values colored.

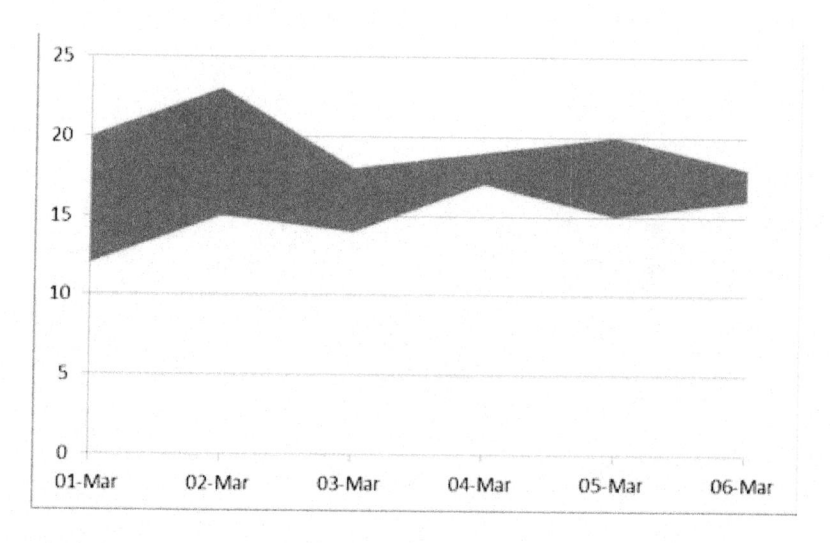

Notes: Sparklines are new and thus not as well-known as other features.

How do I do this?
Answer:
Add a column to show the differences:

	A	B	C	D
1	Date	Low	High	Diff
2	Mar 1	12	20	8
3	Mar 2	15	23	8
4	Mar 3	14	18	4
5	Mar 4	17	19	2
6	Mar 5	15	20	5
7	Mar 6	16	18	2

Then plot columns A, B and D as a stacked bar chart. Finally make the color of the low values transparent.

Notes: A normal area graph won't do it, because if the bottom area is white, you won't get the horizontal gridlines, and if the bottom area is transparent, you'll get the high color throughout.

Switching Axes

188: You have pricing data on products and have asked Excel to produce a graph (automatically). It looks like this:

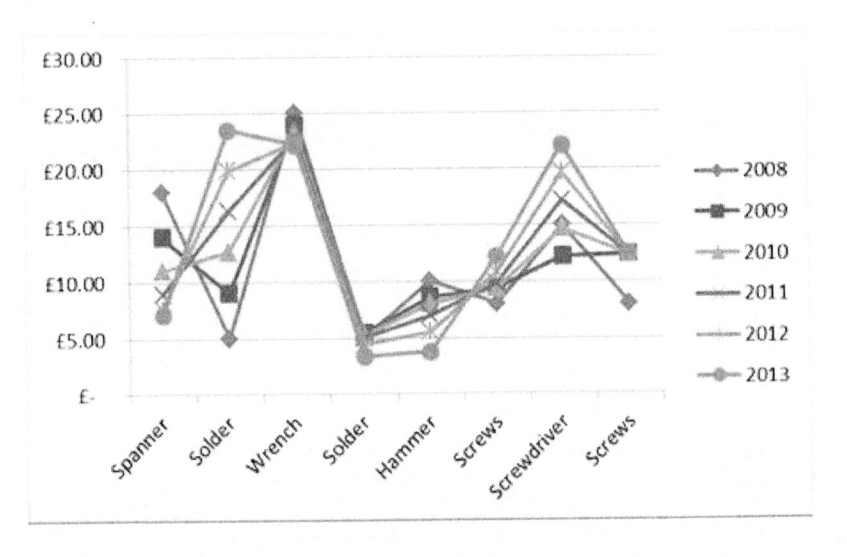

As you really wanted the dates along the bottom and each product as a different line, how would you swap them over?

Answer:
Use the Switch Row/Column in the Design tab:

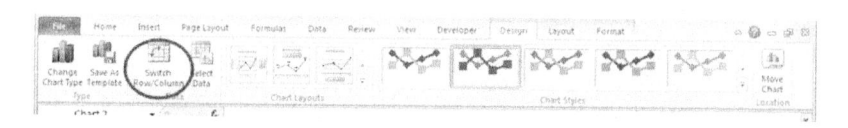

Advanced Excel Interview Questions You'll Most Likely Be Asked   115

Notes: Not as easy in early versions of Excel

Organization Chart

189: I want to use Excel to include an organization chart. What is the easiest way of doing this?
Answer:
Use SmartArt (from the Insert ribbon), then pick Hierarchy and select the organization chart as shown below.

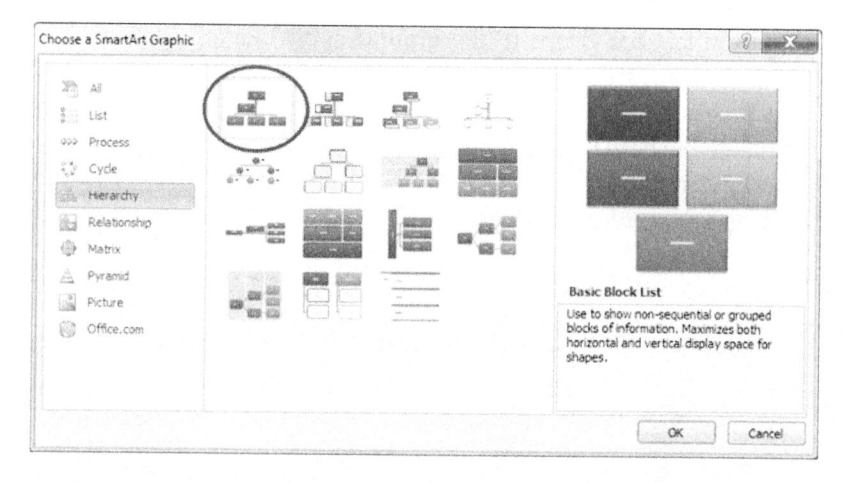

Notes: There are other packages if you are looking for a more complex chart, for example a family tree, but this works fine for a quick and easy org chart.

Waterfalls

190: What is a waterfall (or bridge) graph and how do you create one in Excel? What would a waterfall graph of the following data look like?

	A	B
1	Day	Price
2	Monday	500
3	Tuesday	520
4	Wednesday	490
5	Thursday	530
6	Friday	500
7	Saturday	480

Answer:
A waterfall graph is a column graph where the first bar rises to the start value, the intermediate values show the changes along the way and the last bar drops to the ground, a bit like a bridge with steps across, or a waterfall. You could create one by adding columns for the ends, base, up and down and then creating a stacked bar chart. Change the base bars to no fill, the rises to green and the drops to red. And delete the key.

The graph would look like:

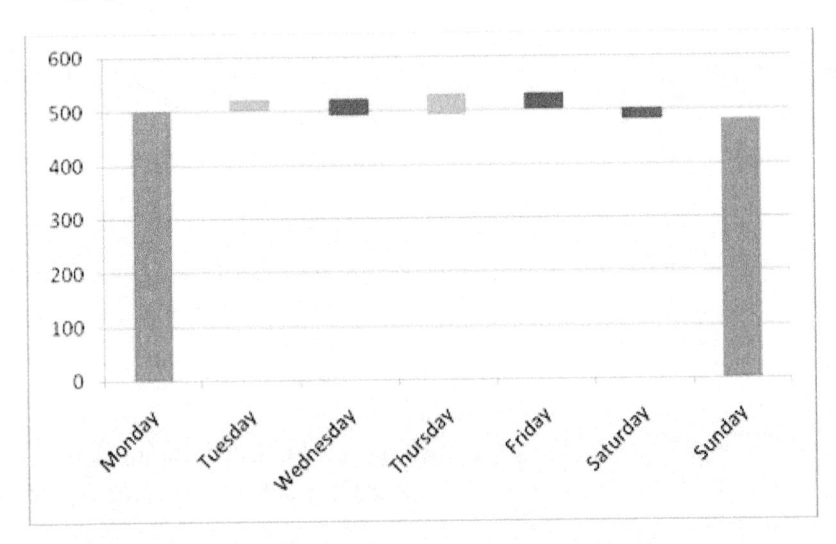

Notes: The final spreadsheet (which you are plotting) would look like this:

	A	B	C	D	E	F
1	Day	Price	Ends	Base	Up	Down
2	Monday	500	500			
3	Tuesday	520		500	20	
4	Wednesday	490		490	0	30
5	Thursday	530		490	40	0
6	Friday	500		500	0	30
7	Saturday	480		480	0	20
8	Sunday		480			

With the formulae being:
In C2:
=B2
In C8
=B7
From D2 to D8:
=IF(C2<>"","",MIN(B2,B1))
From E2 to E8:
=IF(C2<>"","",MIN(D2-D1,0))
From F2 to F8:
=IF(C2<>"","",MAX(B1-B2,0))

Assigning Macros
191: When you right click on a chart, you get the option of Assign Macro..., like this:

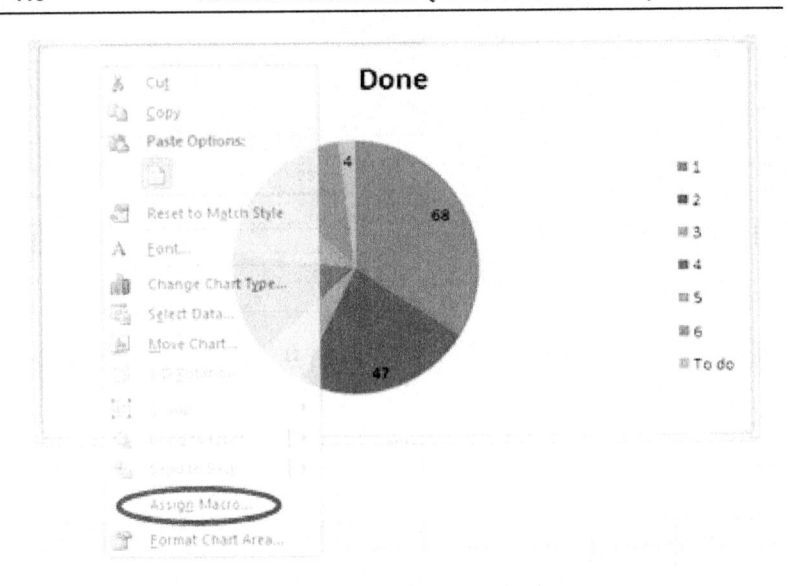

What does it do?

Answer:

It enables a macro to be run whenever the graph is clicked.

Notes: This can be used to pop up a window giving more information, lead to a larger or more detailed version of the graph, print the graph and so on.

HR Questions

Review these typical interview questions and think about how you would answer them. Read the answers listed; you will find best possible answers along with strategies and suggestions.

1: Why did you choose your college major?
Answer:
It's important to display interest in your work, and if your major is related to your current field, it will be simple for you to relate the two. Perhaps you even knew while in college that you wanted to do a job similar to this position, and so you chose the major so as to receive the education and training you needed to succeed. If your major doesn't relate clearly, it's still important to express a sense of passion for your choice, and to specify the importance of pursuing something that matters to you – which is how you made the decision to come to your current career field instead.

2: Tell me about your college experience.
Answer:
It's best to keep this answer positive – don't focus on parties, pizza, or procrastinating. Instead, offer a general summary of the benefits you received in college, followed by an anecdote of a favorite professor or course that opened up your way of thinking about the field you're in. This is a great opportunity for you to show your passion for your career, make sure to answer enthusiastically and confidently.

3: What is the most unique thing about yourself that you would bring to this position?
Answer:
This question is often asked as a close to an interview, and it gives you a final chance to highlight your best qualities to the employer. Treat the question like a sort of review, and explain why your specific mix of education, experience, and passions will be the ideal combination for the employer. Remain confident but humble, and keep your answer to about two minutes.

4: How did your last job stand up to your previous expectations of it?
Answer:
While it's okay to discuss what you learned if you expected too much out of a previous job, it's best to keep this question away from negative statements or portrayals. Focus your answer around what

your previous job did hold that you had expected, and how much you enjoyed those aspects of the position.

5: How did you become interested in this field?
Answer:
This is the chance for you to show your passion for your career – and the interviewer will be assured that you are a great candidate if it's obvious that you enjoy your job. You can include a brief anecdote here in order to make your interest personal, but be sure that it is *brief*. Offer specific names of mentors or professors who aided in your discovery, and make it clear that you love what you do.

6: What was the greatest thing you learned while in school?
Answer:
By offering a lesson you learned outside of the classroom, you can show the interviewer your capacity for creativity, learning, and reflection. The practical lessons you learned in the classroom are certainly invaluable in their own right and may pertain closely to the position, but showing the mastery of a concept that you had to learn on your own will highlight your growth potential.

7: Tell me about a time when you had to learn a different skill set for a new position.
Answer:
Use a specific example to describe what you had to learn and how you set about outlining goals and tasks for yourself. It's important to show that you mastered the skill largely from your dedication to learning it, and because of the systematic approach you took to developing and honing your individual education. Additionally, draw connections between the skill you learned and the new position, and show how well prepared you are for the job.

8: Tell me about a person who has been a great influence in your career.
Answer:
It's important to make this answer easy to relate to – your story should remind the interviewer of the person who was most influential in his or her own career. Explain what you learned from

this person and why they inspired you, and how you hope to model them later in your career with future successes.

9: What would this person tell me about you?
Answer:
Most importantly, if this person is one of your references – they had better know who you are! There are all too many horror stories of professors or past employers being called for a reference, and not being able to recall when they knew you or why you were remarkable, which doesn't send a very positive message to potential employers. This person should remember you as being enthusiastic, passionate, and motivated to learn and succeed.

10: What is the most productive time of day for you?
Answer:
This is a trick question – you should be equally productive all day! While it's normal to become extra motivated for certain projects, and also true that some tasks will require additional work, be sure to emphasize to the interviewer that working diligently throughout the entirety of the day comes naturally to you.

11: What was the most responsibility you were given at your previous job?
Answer:
This question provides you with an opportunity to elaborate on responsibilities that may or may not be on your resume. For instance, your resume may not have allowed room to discuss individual projects you worked on that were really outside the scope of your job responsibilities, but you can tell the interviewer here about the additional work you did and how it translated into new skills and a richer career experience for you.

12: Do you believe you were compensated fairly at your last job?
Answer:
Remember to stay positive, and to avoid making negative comments about your previous employer. If you were not compensated fairly, simply state that you believe your qualities and experience were outside the compensation limitations of the old job, and that you're

looking forward to an opportunity that is more in line with the place you're at in your career.

13: Tell me about a time when you received feedback on your work, and enacted it.
Answer:
Try to give an example of feedback your received early in your career, and the steps you took to incorporate it with your work. The most important part of this question is to display the way you learned from the feedback, as well as your willingness to accept suggestions from your superiors. Be sure to offer reflection and understanding of how the feedback helped your work to improve.

14: Tell me about a time when you received feedback on your work that you did not agree with, or thought was unfair. How did you handle it?
Answer:
When explaining that you did not agree with particular feedback or felt it was unfair, you'll need to justify tactfully why the feedback was inaccurate. Then, explain how you communicated directly with the person who offered the feedback, and, most importantly, how you listened to their response, analyzed it, and then came to a mutual agreement.

15: What was your favorite job, and why?
Answer:
It's best if your favorite job relates to the position you're currently applying for, as you can then easily draw connections between why you enjoyed that job and why you are interested in the current position. Additionally, it is extremely important to explain why you've qualified the particular job as your favorite, and what aspects of it you would look for in another job, so that the interviewer can determine whether or not you are a good fit.

16: Tell me about an opportunity that your last position did not allow you to achieve.
Answer:
Stay focused on the positive, and be understanding of the limitations

of your previous position. Give a specific example of a goal or career objective that you were not able to achieve, but rather than expressing disappointment over the missed opportunity, discuss the ways you're looking forward to the chance to grow in a new position.

17: Tell me about the worst boss you ever had.
Answer:
It's important to keep this answer brief, and positively focused. While you may offer a couple of short, critical assessments of your boss, focus on the things you learned from working with such an individual, and remain sympathetic to challenges the boss may have faced.

18: What are the three most important things you're looking for in a position?
Answer:
The top three things you want in a position should be similar to the top three things the employer wants from an employee, so that it is clear that you are well-matched to the job. For example, the employer wants a candidate who is well-qualified for and has practical experience – and you want a position that allows you to use your education and skills to their best applications. The employer wants a candidate who is willing to take on new challenges and develop new systems to increase sales or productivity – and you want a position that pushes you and offers opportunities to develop, create, and lead new initiatives. The employer wants a candidate who will grow into and stay with the company for a long time – and you want a position that offers stability and believes in building a strong team. Research what the employer is looking for beforehand, and match your objectives to theirs.

19: How are you evaluating the companies you're looking to work with?
Answer:
While you may feel uncomfortable exerting your own requirements during the interview, the employer wants to see that you are thinking critically about the companies you're applying with, just as they are critically looking at you. Don't be afraid to specify what your needs

from a company are (but do try to make sure they match up well with the company – preferably before you apply there), and show confidence and decisiveness in your answer. The interviewer wants to know that you're the kind of person who knows what they want, and how to get it.

20: Are you comfortable working for _____ salary?
Answer:
If the answer to this question is no, it may be a bit of a deal-breaker in a first interview, as you are unlikely to have much room to negotiate. You can try to leverage a bit by highlighting specific experience you have, and how that makes you qualified for more, but be aware that this is very difficult to navigate at this step of the process. To avoid this situation, be aware of industry standards and, if possible, company standards, prior to your application.

21: Why did you choose your last job?
Answer:
In learning what led you to your last job, the interviewer is able to get a feel for the types of things that motivate you. Keep these professionally-focused, and remain passionate about the early points of your career, and how excited you were to get started in the field.

22: How long has it been since your last job and why?
Answer:
Be sure to have an explanation prepared for all gaps in employment, and make sure it's a professional reason. Don't mention difficulties you may have had in finding a job, and instead focus on positive things such as pursuing outside interests or perhaps returning to school for additional education.

23: What other types of jobs have you been looking for?
Answer:
The answer to this question can show the interviewer that you're both on the market and in demand. Mention jobs you've applied for or looked at that are closely related to your field, or similar to the position you're interviewing for. Don't bring up last-ditch efforts that found you applying for a part-time job completely unrelated to your

field.

24: Have you ever been disciplined at work?
Answer:
Hopefully the answer here is no – but if you have been disciplined for something at work though, be absolutely sure that you can explain it thoroughly. Detail what you learned from the situation, and reflect on how you grew after the process.

25: What is your availability like?
Answer:
Your availability should obviously be as open as possible, and any gaps in availability should be explained and accounted for. Avoid asking about vacation or personal days (as well as other benefits), and convey to the interviewer how serious you are about your work.

26: May I contact your current employer?
Answer:
If possible, it is best to allow an interviewer to contact your current employer as a reference. However, if it's important that your employer is not contacted, explain your reason tactfully, such as you just started job searching and you haven't had the opportunity yet to inform them that you are looking for other employment. Be careful of this reasoning though, as employers may wonder if you'll start shopping for something better while employed with them as well.

27: Do you have any valuable contacts you could bring to our business?
Answer:
It's great if you can bring knowledge, references, or other contacts that your new employer may be able to network with. However, be sure that you aren't offering up any of your previous employer's clients, or in any way violating contractual agreements.

28: How soon would you be available to start working?
Answer:
While you want to be sure that you're available to start as soon as possible if the company is interested in hiring you, if you still have

another job, be sure to give them at least two weeks' notice. Though your new employer may be anxious for you to start, they will want to hire a worker whom they can respect for giving adequate notice, so that they won't have to worry if you'll eventually leave them in the lurch.

29: Why would your last employer say that you left?
Answer:
The key to this question is that your employer's answer must be the same as your own answer about why you left. For instance, if you've told your employer that you left to find a position with greater opportunities for career advancement, your employer had better not say that you were let go for missing too many days of work. Honesty is key in your job application process.

30: How long have you been actively looking for a job?
Answer:
It's best if you haven't been actively looking for a job for very long, as a long period of time may make the interviewer wonder why no one else has hired you. If it has been awhile, make sure to explain why, and keep it positive. Perhaps you haven't come across many opportunities that provide you with enough of a challenge or that are adequately matched to someone of your education and experience.

31: When don't you show up to work?
Answer:
Clearly, the only time acceptable to miss work is for a real emergency or when you're truly sick – so don't start bringing up times now that you plan to miss work due to vacations or family birthdays. Alternatively, you can tell the interviewer how dedicated to your work you are, and how you always strive to be fully present and to put in the same amount of work every time you come in, even when you're feeling slightly under the weather.

32: What is the most common reason you miss work?
Answer:
If there is a reason that you will miss work routinely, this is the time to disclose it – but doing so during an interview will reflect

negatively on you. Ideally, you will only miss work during cases of extreme illness or other emergencies.

33: What is your attendance record like?
Answer:
Be sure to answer this question honestly, but ideally you will have already put in the work to back up the fact that you rarely miss days or arrive late. However, if there are gaps in your attendance, explain them briefly with appropriate reasons, and make sure to emphasize your dedication to your work, and reliability.

34: Where did you hear about this position?
Answer:
This may seem like a simple question, but the answer can actually speak volumes about you. If you were referred by a friend or another employee who works for the company, this is a great chance to mention your connection (if the person is in good standing!). However, if you heard about it from somewhere like a career fair or a work placement agency, you may want to focus on how pleased you were to come across such a wonderful opportunity.

35: Tell me anything else you'd like me to know when making a hiring decision.
Answer:
This is a great opportunity for you to give a final sell of yourself to the interviewer – use this time to remind the interviewer of why you are qualified for the position, and what you can bring to the company that no one else can. Express your excitement for the opportunity to work with a company pursuing *X mission*.

36: Where do you find ideas?
Answer:
Ideas can come from all places, and an interviewer wants to see that your ideas are just as varied. Mention multiple places that you gain ideas from, or settings in which you find yourself brainstorming. Additionally, elaborate on how you record ideas or expand upon them later.

37: How do you achieve creativity in the workplace?

Answer:
It's important to show the interviewer that you're capable of being resourceful and innovative in the workplace, without stepping outside the lines of company values. Explain where ideas normally stem from for you (examples may include an exercise such as list-making or a mind map), and connect this to a particular task in your job that it would be helpful to be creative in.

38: How do you push others to create ideas?
Answer:
If you're in a supervisory position, this may be requiring employees to submit a particular number of ideas, or to complete regular idea-generating exercises, in order to work their creative muscles. However, you can also push others around you to create ideas simply by creating more of your own. Additionally, discuss with the interviewer the importance of questioning people as a way to inspire ideas and change.

39: Describe your creativity.
Answer:
Try to keep this answer within the professional realm, but if you have an impressive background in something creative outside of your employment history, don't be afraid to include it in your answer also. The best answers about creativity will relate problem-solving skills, goal-setting, and finding innovative ways to tackle a project or make a sale in the workplace. However, passions outside of the office are great, too (so long as they don't cut into your work time or mental space).

40: How would you handle a negative coworker?
Answer:
Everyone has to deal with negative coworkers – and the single best way to do so is to remain positive. You may try to build a relationship with the coworker or relate to them in some way, but even if your efforts are met with a cold shoulder, you must retain your positive attitude. Above all, stress that you would never allow a coworker's negativity to impact your own work or productivity.

41: What would you do if you witnessed a coworker surfing the web, reading a book, etc, wasting company time?
Answer:
The interviewer will want to see that you realize how detrimental it is for employees to waste company time, and that it is not something you take lightly. Explain the way you would adhere to company policy, whether that includes talking to the coworker yourself, reporting the behavior straight to a supervisor, or talking to someone in HR.

42: How do you handle competition among yourself and other employees?
Answer:
Healthy competition can be a great thing, and it is best to stay focused on the positive aspects of this here. Don't bring up conflict among yourself and other coworkers, and instead focus on the motivation to keep up with the great work of others, and the ways in which coworkers may be a great support network in helping to push you to new successes.

43: When is it okay to socialize with coworkers?
Answer:
This question has two extreme answers (all the time, or never), and your interviewer, in most cases, will want to see that you fall somewhere in the middle. It's important to establish solid relationships with your coworkers, but never at the expense of getting work done. Ideally, relationship-building can happen with exercises of teamwork and special projects, as well as in the break room.

44: Tell me about a time when a major change was made at your last job, and how you handled it.
Answer:
Provide a set-up for the situation including the old system, what the change was, how it was implemented, and the results of the change, and include how you felt about each step of the way. Be sure that your initial thoughts on the old system are neutral, and that your excitement level grows with each step of the new change, as an

interviewer will be pleased to see your adaptability.

45: When delegating tasks, how do you choose which tasks go to which team members?
Answer:
The interviewer is looking to gain insight into your thought process with this question, so be sure to offer thorough reasoning behind your choice. Explain that you delegate tasks based on each individual's personal strengths, or that you look at how many other projects each person is working on at the time, in order to create the best fit possible.

46: Tell me about a time when you had to stand up for something you believed strongly about to coworkers or a supervisor.
Answer:
While it may be difficult to explain a situation of conflict to an interviewer, this is a great opportunity to display your passions and convictions, and your dedication to your beliefs. Explain not just the situation to the interviewer, but also elaborate on why it was so important to you to stand up for the issue, and how your coworker or supervisor responded to you afterward – were they more respectful? Unreceptive? Open-minded? Apologetic?

47: Tell me about a time when you helped someone finish their work, even though it wasn't "your job."
Answer:
Though you may be frustrated when required to pick up someone else's slack, it's important that you remain positive about lending a hand. The interviewer will be looking to see if you're a team player, and by helping someone else finish a task that he or she couldn't manage alone, you show both your willingness to help the team succeed, and your own competence.

48: What are the challenges of working on a team? How do you handle this?
Answer:
There are many obvious challenges to working on a team, such as handling different perspectives, navigating individual schedules, or

accommodating difficult workers. It's best to focus on one challenge, such as individual team members missing deadlines or failing to keep commitments, and then offer a solution that clearly addresses the problem. For example, you could organize weekly status meetings for your team to discuss progress, or assign shorter deadlines in order to keep the long-term deadline on schedule.

49: Do you value diversity in the workplace?
Answer:
Diversity is important in the workplace in order to foster an environment that is accepting, equalizing, and full of different perspectives and backgrounds. Be sure to show your awareness of these issues, and stress the importance of learning from others' experiences.

50: How would you handle a situation in which a coworker was not accepting of someone else's diversity?
Answer:
Explain that it is important to adhere to company policies regarding diversity, and that you would talk to the relevant supervisors or management team. When it is appropriate, it could also be best to talk to the coworker in question about the benefits of alternate perspectives – if you can handle the situation yourself, it's best not to bring resolvable issues to management.

51: Are you rewarded more from working on a team, or accomplishing a task on your own?
Answer:
It's best to show a balance between these two aspects – your employer wants to see that you're comfortable working on your own, and that you can complete tasks efficiently and well without assistance. However, it's also important for your employer to see that you can be a team player, and that you understand the value that multiple perspectives and efforts can bring to a project.

And Finally Good Luck!

INDEX

Advanced Excel Interview Questions

General Questions

1: If you have bought one copy of Microsoft Excel 2010 and have installed it on your computer, under what conditions are you allowed to install it on a second machine?

2: In real life, leap years are divisible by 4 but not by 100 unless they are also divisible by 400. So we get:
What does Excel do with these years (i.e. is there a 29th February in these years in Excel)?

3: What is the shortcut key to insert a new worksheet into the workbook?

4: I have been working on my spreadsheet for some time and now suddenly when I press the down arrow, the current cell does not move down one cell, but the whole spreadsheet moves up one cell on the screen. So my cursor, which was originally on cell B5 is still on cell B5. What has happened and how do I fix it?

5: You want to put the current time into cell B4 and the current date into cell C4 (as static text, so that they won't change as time passes). What is the quickest way of doing this?

6: In the following picture, what is the user doing?

7: You have a list of locations for your fifty shops. You will often need the list put into spreadsheets. What method can you use to speedily put them in when you need them? Where would you find this functionality?

8: Obviously you could use borders to change the colors of any of the edges of the cells, but (without using borders), how do you change the colors of all the gridlines?

9: When would you enable iterative calculations?

10: What happens if, after typing the following formula into cell A8, you press Control + Enter, instead of just Enter?

11: You have a large spreadsheet - many rows and columns. What are these keyboard shortcuts for?

12: When you set your print area, it is the trigger for Excel to show you the Page Breaks. How do you put an icon onto the Quick Access Toolbar to turn these Page Breaks on and off?

13: Without using form controls, how do you create a drop-down list in a cell?

14: You have the number 125 in the current cell (which is quite wide). What happens when you click the highlighted button on the home page?

15: What is a circular reference?

16: Which of the following platforms is a version of Microsoft Excel available for?

17: What is the difference between a database and a spreadsheet?

18: You have a large spreadsheet (many rows and columns) and are in the middle of it when you need to enter a new line. What is the quickest way of getting to the start of the next empty row at the bottom of the spreadsheet?

19: In the following spreadsheet: You are on cell B3. What is the first thing that happens if you select Table from the Insert ribbon?

20: On the Insert ribbon, there is a button to insert Slicers. What are slicers?

21: How do I add my own commands on to a ribbon?

22: What are the basic hardware requirements for Excel 2010?

23: At the bottom of a spreadsheet, it says the word "Calculate", like this: What does it mean, and how can it be affected?

24: If you want to format a cell as locked: What do you have to do the cell? What action do you also have to take?

25: I put the year 2008 into cell A1. However when I drag down, it doesn't give me 2009, 2010 and so on but puts 2008 into every cell. How do I change it so that it gives me 2009, etc.?

26: What is the keyboard shortcut for turning on data filtering for the current area?

27: What does the "From Web" button do?

28: What are ScreenTips, and how can you turn them ON/OFF?

29: You have a column of data. There is a sort button that allows you to sort it into ascending order or descending order. So what does the "custom" sort do?

30: You have a large spreadsheet with many rows and columns. Is it possible to keep the column headings on the screen even when you scroll down so you can still see which column is which?

31: I have a document with pages from 1 to 50. I would like the spreadsheet to follow this, and thus the page numbers in the footer to count from 51. How do I set the start number for the page numbers?

32: You are working on a small screen. Is there an easy way of turning off the ribbons?

33: If you run Windows in Safe Mode, can you still use Microsoft Excel? Could you use previous versions of Microsoft Excel?

34: How do I show two worksheets in the same workbook side by side?

35: List which versions (e.g. Professional) of Microsoft Office 2010 come with Microsoft Excel.

36: You are designing a spreadsheet where it would be preferable if the column headings went down instead of up (as shown below). Is it possible to do this and, if so, how?

37: How is it possible to perform Menu and Ribbon options using just the keyboard, and how would you figure out which key you need for each option?

38: When aligning text, the usual options of Left, Centered, Right and Justified are all there. But what are Fill and Distributed alignments? For example if we have the following cells left justified, how would they appear if they were aligned using Fill or Distributed?

39: You are planning to move house, and want to create an Excel spreadsheet with all the tasks you need to do and the status of each (with probably some notes somewhere). Where do you start?

40: You are editing a formula and it is so long it goes off the end of the formula line. What is the keyboard shortcut for expanding the formula bar?

41: What sort of Excel spreadsheets can't be shared so that multiple people can open the same spreadsheet at the same time?

42: In a spreadsheet, many of the cells have been highlighted, made bold or had their colors changed as people have worked on them. I would like to bring them all back to plain black text on a white background with no bold or highlighting. What is the easiest way of doing this?

43: I am producing a balance sheet. All numbers I have entered are full amounts of currency, e.g. 12045.25 for $12,045.25. However the balance sheet requires all numbers to be in multiples of 1,000, so the above number would just appear as 12. How do I divide all the monetary numbers by 1,000 without creating another whole set of cells? Note I don't want the current year or other non-financial numbers divided by 12.

44: You have a spreadsheet but have forgotten the password. What can you do?

45: I am printing a sheet for my students. I want them to see the row and column headings when I print my spreadsheet. How can I do this?

46: Nearly all of my Excel workbooks are just one sheet. How do I reconfigure Excel so that when I create a new workbook it only has 1 worksheet by default?

47: In Word, I had styles such as Heading 1, Heading 2 and Heading 3 which I used to identify main sections in my document. Does Excel have anything similar to this?

48: Some of my columns are too narrow to see all the text, while the Age column is wider than it needs to be. Give atleast two ways I can resize all my columns to fit the text.

49: What is Microsoft Office Backstage and of what relevance is it to Excel?

50: What are the shortcut keys for formatting selected cells as either currency (e.g. $4.30) or percentage (e.g. 36%)?

51: How do you enable automatic saving of Excel documents and adjust how often they are saved?

52: If I create a document in Microsoft Excel 2010, and then try and load it in Microsoft Excel Starter 2010, what files can load? What functionality will still work?

53: You would like a key combination to be able to show the office clipboard. You could write a macro or assign a key, but what key combination does Excel offer to show you the office clipboard? As it is turned off by default, how would you enable it?

54: You find it easier to read text on a darker background, as shown. How can you change this within Excel and what will it affect (e.g. will it affect new spreadsheets you create)?

55: If you want to export your spreadsheet to people who may have an earlier version of Excel, how do you find out what functionality will be lost and what may appear differently?

56: Your company has a list of words (including the company's name) which should be accepted as valid "words" for the Excel spell checker. How can you add these words to the spell checker so it doesn't flag them every time it is used?

57: What is the difference between underlining and accounting underlining?

58: When formatting a cell, what are "Special" formats (see below)?

59: If you prefer using the keyboard, what key combination moves the focus from the worksheet to get you to the ribbon and what is the sequence?

60: How do I tell Excel to print my spreadsheet right in the middle of the page?

61: How do you tell Excel that you want the size of the text in a cell to be small enough so that the text fits in the cell, even if the column is later made wider or narrower?

62: When debugging a spreadsheet, one factor that is useful is to highlight all cells with formulae in them. What is the quickest way of highlighting all cells with formulae in?

63: How do you put a trademark symbol after a product name in Excel (without having to go to Insert Symbol and finding it)?

64: How do you get Excel to show if capslock or numlock is currently pressed?

65: What is the camera tool, and where would you find it?

Formulae

66: In the above spreadsheet you decide to write an array formula to find the total cost of all the animals. What is the formula you would use and how would you identify to Excel that it is an array formula?

67: With the sheet shown below, what is the simplest formula to work out the number of seconds elapsed between the date and time that the process started and when it ended?

68: With reference to the above table, what would you get from the following formulae?

69: In the below spreadsheet: If I have a cell (D4) with 121 in it, I can use vlookup to give me the product's name. The question is if the cell D4 has the name of the product (e.g. "Butter"), how do I write the formula to find the product's ID?

70: In my local league, the score of each person is recorded. As the scoring system works, no two people can have the same score. I want the spreadsheet to identify who is currently in first, second and third place. Thus I want a formula to go into B2 (which can be dragged down to B4 without changing it) to give me the names of who is currently in each place. What is the simplest formula to do it?

71: You have a spreadsheet like this: You are typing in a formula into cell C2 for the tax. You realize that when you click on the cell B5 for the tax, Excel put in a relative cell reference instead of the absolute one you really wanted as you plan to drag this formula down the column. What is the easiest way to convert this reference in B5 to an absolute reference?

72: Is there anything wrong with this formula and, if so, what is it?

73: What does the following formula do?

74: Working with the following spreadsheet (on sheet1): As you would expect, it displays as: The question is: How will it display after you have sorted column 1 (into ascending order)?

75: What does the following formula do?

76: In Excel, what are precedents, and how do you get to see them?

77: The Find function allows you to find a set of characters in a cell, for example to find "jumps" in "the quick brown fox jumps over the lazy dog". However what if you are searching for a word and don't want your formula to pick it up in another word. For example "pen" in "the pen is mighty" will be found but it will not trigger in "metalwork and carpentry". You can't guarantee that there are spaces round it as there may be punctuation marks around. How do you find if the word you are looking for is there? Assume cell A1 has the phrase and B1 has the word you are looking for, what do you put into C1 to show if B1 is a word in A1?

78: What formula would find all cells in the named range "data" where the value starts with the letter "t" or "T"?

79: You had a formula to average the set of students' marks, which was: However you now want to discard the lowest and highest marks and just average the rest. What formula would you now use?

80: In the spreadsheet below, a formula was put into cell D2 and dragged down. What reason(s) could there be for the cell D3 showing an error?

81: With the following spreadsheet: And so on down columns A, B and C (the last row will keep changing as more data are added).How would you write the COUNTIFS formula to find out how much sales Fred has made in the last year? (Don't worry about leap years)

82: In a spreadsheet, cell A1 contains the person's user ID. Then cell B1 has the following. What is this formula doing?

83: I have imported some data and column A has the dates in. I have inserted a new column to the left and want to put the day of the week into it. What's the simplest way of doing this?

84: You want to put into cell B1 "House Prices 2012". To ensure it wraps correctly, you want to put a return into the cell (to have 2 lines of text in the cell). Is it possible and, if so, how?

85: In a spreadsheet, there is column A with cities and states in them. The person has them on 2 lines with a line break between them. You want to convert them to the format "City, State". What formula do you put into B1 (and then drag down) to do this?

86: What does the CLEAN() function do?

87: What does the following formula do?

88: A column has text in it that is not lined up. You have tracked it down to the fact that there a variable number of spaces in front of the text in each cell. If the cells affected are A1 to A200, what formula would you put into cell A2 (and then drag down) to get rid of these spaces?

89: In the following spreadsheet, why is the sum at the bottom of the column showing 0?

90: On my spreadsheet, the first worksheet is called "Raw Data". On cell A1 on sheet 2, how do I say that the contents of this cell should be the same as that on cell A1 on the first sheet?

91: In the following spreadsheet: What is wrong with the following formula for the cell D1?

92: Is it possible to get Excel to tell you whenever you have entered a formula that uses a cell which is empty?

93: You have the exact time for an event in cell A1. What formula would you write to round this time to the nearest 15 minutes?

94: What does the following formula do?

95: You have a complex spreadsheet, not huge but many calculations all over the place. How is it possible to show the original formulae in the cells rather than the numbers that they calculate?

96: I want to calculate the results of adding C4 and C5 and then multiplying the result by C6, but only if there is some data in cells C2, C4 and B1. What is the formula for doing this?

97: How do you change all years to show which decade they are in? For example: Just give the formula for cell B2, in a form that can be dragged down to B5.

98: A complex sheet has a cell with a long formula in cell C4 (with filled cells al around). How do you break down the formula to figure out what it is doing?

99: If I have a formula in C1 that divides one number by another: I could test if A1 was 0 and then only divide if it is non-zero. However I actually have a much more complex formula with many divisions, any one of which could generate the error. So the question is, how do I write a (short) formula for the first example which does not have to check if A1 is zero before doing the calculation?

100: Cell A1 has a date. What formula would be needed to return the number of days in the month that A1 falls. For example if A1 had January 10th, 1993; the result would be 31, because January 1993 had 31 days.

101: I have a column which shows the height or ornaments to the nearest inch. They are currently numbers converted from centimetres, e.g. 14.803. I would like them displayed to the nearest whole number followed by the inch sign, e.g. 15". How do I do this?

102: I have a named range that is defined like this: What area does it refer to?

103: I am looking for low cost online tutorials for Microsoft Excel. Where is a good place to start looking?

104: You have written a formula including the function vlookup, but it isn't working as expected. Give three possible reasons for this

105: I have a column and want to find the lowest number. Is there a button in Excel which will do this for me?

106: You are working out interest payments and have selected the function PMT (as shown below), but need to look something up in the Help system. What is the quickest way of finding Help on this function?

107: You have a spreadsheet and you want to add a formula to the bottom of each column that averages all the values. You select the empty row that the formula is going to go in and type in the formula for the first column: What is the easiest way to get this one formula to be applied to all the columns?

108: You have a spreadsheet like the one below. At the bottom of the column you would normally put the average. However there are occasions when there could be an extreme value which would distort the data. So you want to just average the middle numbers (i.e. excluding the highest and lowest number). What formula do you use (for cell B8)?

109: If you are on a cell with a formula, what key would you normally press to edit the formula in the cell? Also, what would happen if this key does not work and, instead takes you to the formula bar?

110: I have the following spreadsheet: where all dates are entered as dates (not as text). Our company works on Mondays to Fridays only. I want to find the number of working days between today and the deadline. In addition, the company will close on Monday 17th to Tuesday 18th September for its national conference, and also Wednesday the 4th of July and the first Monday

in September are national holidays. What formula do I put into cell B3?
111: I work on shifts, taking Tuesday and Wednesdays off each week. What formula do I use to find out how many days there are from now to the end of December (just put the current year in)? Note that the current date will change, so we will need the function for this as well.
112: What does the function edate() do?

Problems

113: Using just a single conditional format, how do you create a chessboard pattern of alternating black and white cells?
114: You want to use Excel to create a calendar for next year, with your photos above each month. How would you do this?
115: You live in a country where a comma shows thousands and a full stop is the decimal point. For example 1234½ would be shown as 1,234.5. However you have been sent a comma separated text file from Spain, where it is the other way round - so 1234½ would be seen as 1.234,5. So the file could look like: How do you import this data?
116: In cell A1, you have a time, in the form hh:mm (for example 10:45). If you had a normal analog clock, the hour hand would be between the 10 and 11, and the minute hand would be on the 9. What formula can you put into cell B1 to show the angle between the clock hands?
117: You have a long column of values. Without sorting the values, how can you highlight any values that are duplicated?
118: The numbers on a snakes and ladders board go backwards and forwards like this: The formula which would be written in every cell and would generate these numbers was written as (formatted to make it easier to read): What is wrong with the formula and how should it be correctly written?
119: You have a column of your spreadsheet with temperatures typed in as numbers. However you want to show them as temperatures with ° F after them. How do you do this (including how you get the degree sign)?
120: You have submitted your budget proposal in an Excel spreadsheet to your boss and he has used the drawing tool to put a red line through every item he wants removed. What is the easiest way of automatically removing these items?
121: I have a spreadsheet of US names and addresses. In column H is their Zip code (a five-digit number). I want to ensure that whenever this row is entered, there is always 5 digits put in. What is the easiest way of doing this?
122: You have numbers in the column from B2 to B9. You are in cell B10. What is the quickest way of putting a formula into cell B10 to sum the cells above (i.e. fewest key presses)?
123: IP (Internet protocol) addresses should be of the form 192.168.001.125. In other words there should be a full stop between each three digit set. How do

Advanced Excel Interview Questions You'll Most Likely Be Asked   141

I show this in an Excel cell (without converting the number to text)?
124: You have several options which can be adjusted, and need the values that give you the best result. What set of Excel functionality would you use for this and where would you find it?

VBA / Coding

125: One of the features of hiding a sheet is that another user can just come along and unhide it. How can you hide a sheet such that someone else can't just unhide it? What code would you use to apply this to Sheet1? If it is hidden such that they can't unhide it, can they still get the data from it?
126: When writing VBA in Excel, how do you turn off the automatic syntax checking of your code?
127: Is the default for macros to use relative, absolute or other references? Also, how do you change from one form to another?
128: Often when you are using Excel to create an application, you want to turn off many of the Excel features so that users can focus on the functionality you have coded in. What VBA code would you use to turn off the ribbon?
129: In the following code: If you are debugging the subroutine, which line will be highlighted when the user presses F8 once?
130: What does the following code do?
131: How do you store macros so that you can use them in any spreadsheet?
132: In your VBA code, you want to check for cells content, but you don't mind if there are capital letters instead of lowercase (or vice versa). What code would you use to make the comparisons case insensitive?
133: When you create a macro in the personal workbook, you can create it without a problem. You can also run it. However what happens (by default) when you try to edit it and how do you fix it?
134: In VBA, how do you change the number of spaces that are put in for each time TAB is pressed?
135: The following function has not been commented. What does it do?
136: In my VBA, I have the code: What is the range of values for LittleNumber?
137: In VBA, how do you find the dimensions of the current Excel window?
138: In VBA, how do you check if the file c:\output.txt already exists?
139: You are writing VBA which will ask a question: You want there to be a question mark symbol, an OK button and a Cancel button. How should the line of code end?
140: You want your code to delay for 30 minutes before starting (because you have triggered other code which may take up to 30 minutes to generate the data that Excel will be importing). What VBA instruction(s) would you use to generate the 30 minute delay?
141: What does the following code do?

142: I have an Excel worksheet with a macro. How do I create a button that runs that macro?

143: What does the following code do?

144: One computer has all macros enabled. As this could be a security risk (because a macro could do anything), you want to turn this back to the default where macros are normally disabled but with the user notified. How do you do this?

145: What is the preferred method of binding? Which method of binding is fastest?

146: I have text in cells from A2 to A22. What formula do I need to calculate the total number of characters in these cells?

147: I start to record a macro and ask for it to be stored in my Personal Marco Workbook: What is the filename of the file that will hold my macro?

148: When does the following code run?

149 In the options below: if Require Variable Declaration is ticked, what words will be put at the start of any new module?

Specific Uses

150: You have a column of numbers and want to do a variety of basis analysis to understand what data you have, such as sum, mean, minimum and standard deviation. What alternative is there to typing in a separate formula for each one?

151: You want to work out the monthly repayments on a loan of $1000, borrowed for 5 years at 5% APR, as shown below (all numbers were entered as numbers and then reformatted as shown below). What formula would you write to calculate how much each repayment is?

152: In the spreadsheet below, the value in column B is one sixth of the value of column A. What is the simplest way of generating the fractions as shown below?

153: I am using Excel to prepare a school timetable. I have one sheet named for each of "Geography", "History", "General Science", "Religious-Education", "English", "PE" and so on. What is the problem?

154: What is the difference between workbook and worksheet protection?

155: I need to calculate tax. The way the tax works is as follows: if the person earns up to $5,000, they pay 10% tax. If they earn between $5,000 and $50,000, they pay 10% on the first $5,000 and then 20% on the rest. And if they earn over $50,000, they pay 10% on the first $5,000, 20% on the bit up to $50,000 and then 25% on the rest. So my initial spreadsheet looks like this (all numbers entered as numbers and then formatted): As any of the numbers may change, they should all be referred to by cell. Fortunately any changes will not change the number of rates (from three).
What formula should be in cell B7?

Advanced Excel Interview Questions You'll Most Likely Be Asked   143

156: In the following spreadsheet, the products have been laid out horizontally. We want them so that they are all in one column, with the first row initially and then the next and so on, i.e. and so on. We have allocated sheet2 for this sorted data. What formula do we put into Sheet2!A1 to drag down and sort all the data for us (i.e. without changing the source data)?

157: The membership list for my association looks like this: Luckily, all the data in column A has been entered in the format of title, first name and lastname (as shown). I will want to do sorting on last name, and some mail merging, so I want each of these in separate columns. This is the titles in column A, the firstnames in column B and the lastnames in column C. What is the easiest way of doing this?

158: What VBA is needed to specify a header on the current Excel worksheet as the following?

159: You have written a spreadsheet in Microsoft Excel 2010 using statistical functions that were all available in Excel 2003. However when you ship it to your colleague in Microsoft Excel 2003, he complains that some of his results are different from yours. Give two possible causes.

160: How long will it take to pay off a $12,000 loan at $400 per month, with interest at 0.5% per month? What formula should I put into cell B4?

161: Where is the icon - or where are the icons - which allow you to start recording a macro?

162: How do you get a macro to automatically run as soon as Excel loads the workbook?

163: You have a macro that runs automatically when Excel loads the workbook. How do you stop it from running as a one-off or for the future?

164: I can afford to pay $1,000 per month for a house, and I expect to pay it for the next 30 years. If the interest rate on the mortgage is 5% per year, I want to find what value of a house I can afford. Ignoring other numbers such as insurance and taxes, what formula should I put into B4?

165: You want to list the features of two products, like this: How do you put the ticks and crosses in?

166: In our local dice game, we need to roll four dice and then add up the highest three. I have created an Excel spreadsheet. What formula would I need for cell B1 to get a random number from 1 to 6 (so that I can drag it down to B2:B4)? What is the simplest formula for B5 to add up the highest of the dice in the cells above?

167: The formula for the area of a circle is: , where r is the radius. If the radius of a circle is in cell A1, what is the formula for the area of that circle?

Graphs, Drawing and Pictures

168: What is a polar chart and when would you use it?

169: When saving your spreadsheet, it is huge. You have not that much data or formulae in, so it must be down to those high quality pictures you put in and then shrunk. As this spreadsheet will only be printed on a standard laser printer, how can you reduce the resolution of the graphics so that the file size is reduced?

170: You have a chart on the current worksheet. However now you want to move it so that it is on a sheet of its own. How do you do this?

171: I have a picture in my spreadsheet (the picture on the left) and I want to blur the edges (to get the picture on the right). Which of the Microsoft Office / Windows programs should I transfer it into to blur the edges and how do I do it?

172: Our sales report over the years 2009-2011 looks like this: We want to circle all quarters where sales were over $300,000 (as shown). How can we get Excel to do this without having to do each one manually?

173: I have a spreadsheet as below and want to add a Gandtt chart (as shown). How do I create the floating brown bars?

174: What types of data values cannot be shown on a Doughnut graph?

175: I want to draw a circle on my spreadsheet using shapes. How do I do this?

176: I have a graph of 4 points, where (as you would expect) all the points show up in the same color. What is the easiest way of making each of them a different color - as shown below?

177: You have a spreadsheet such as the one below. What is the quickest way of graphing the data (i.e. to produce the graph shown)?

178: I have a worksheet which shows the personal details of a person. One of the details is in cell B4 – it is the filename of their picture, all files being stored in the directory c:\pictures. I have an image (called image1) for the picture to be shown in. What VBA code do I need to do to put their picture onto the screen?

179: My pictures on my spreadsheet are not printing in color. What Excel setting might I have done to cause this and how can I turn it off?

180: What are Drop lines and how are they added to a graph?

181: You have selected an area of cells. What is the shortcut key to:

182: What types of trend lines does Microsoft Excel support directly (i.e. without having to write them yourself)?

183: I have a graph showing sales for each employee: I want to simplify the graph to just show the number of thousands of dollars (rather than the full amount including cents). How can I easily do this?

184: In sparklines, which points can you ask to be shown to draw attention to them (e.g. the highest?)

185: You have a graph with multiple lines, but would prefer the key to be below the graph instead of to the right. What is the easiest way of moving them?

186: If each column represents a year earlier than the previous (rather than the next year which is more common), how can you get the sparklines to show the data with time going forwards?

187: I want a graph, showing the horizontal gridlines, but only the area between the two values colored. How do I do this?

188: You have pricing data on products and have asked Excel to produce a graph (automatically). It looks like this: As you really wanted the dates along the bottom and each product as a different line, how would you swap them over?

189: I want to use Excel to include an organization chart. What is the easiest way of doing this?

190: What is a waterfall (or bridge) graph and how do you create one in Excel? What would a waterfall graph of the following data look like?

191: When you right click on a chart, you get the option of Assign Macro..., like this: What does it do?

HR Questions

1: Why did you choose your college major?
2: Tell me about your college experience.
3: What is the most unique thing about yourself that you would bring to this position?
4: How did your last job stand up to your previous expectations of it?
5: How did you become interested in this field?
6: What was the greatest thing you learned while in school?
7: Tell me about a time when you had to learn a different skill set for a new position.
8: Tell me about a person who has been a great influence in your career.
9: What would this person tell me about you?
10: What is the most productive time of day for you?
11: What was the most responsibility you were given at your previous job?
12: Do you believe you were compensated fairly at your last job?
13: Tell me about a time when you received feedback on your work, and enacted it.
14: Tell me about a time when you received feedback on your work that you did not agree with, or thought was unfair. How did you handle it?
15: What was your favorite job, and why?
16: Tell me about an opportunity that your last position did not allow you to achieve.
17: Tell me about the worst boss you ever had.
18: What are the three most important things you're looking for in a position?
19: How are you evaluating the companies you're looking to work with?
20: Are you comfortable working for _____ salary?
21: Why did you choose your last job?
22: How long has it been since your last job and why?
23: What other types of jobs have you been looking for?
24: Have you ever been disciplined at work?
25: What is your availability like?
26: May I contact your current employer?
27: Do you have any valuable contacts you could bring to our business?
28: How soon would you be available to start working?
29: Why would your last employer say that you left?
30: How long have you been actively looking for a job?
32: What is the most common reason you miss work?
33: What is your attendance record like?
34: Where did you hear about this position?
35: Tell me anything else you'd like me to know when making a hiring decision.
36: Where do you find ideas?

37: How do you achieve creativity in the workplace?
38: How do you push others to create ideas?
39: Describe your creativity.
40: How would you handle a negative coworker?
41: What would you do if you witnessed a coworker surfing the web, reading a book, etc, wasting company time?
42: How do you handle competition among yourself and other employees?
43: When is it okay to socialize with coworkers?
44: Tell me about a time when a major change was made at your last job, and how you handled it.
45: When delegating tasks, how do you choose which tasks go to which team members?
46: Tell me about a time when you had to stand up for something you believed strongly about to coworkers or a supervisor.
47: Tell me about a time when you helped someone finish their work, even though it wasn't "your job."
48: What are the challenges of working on a team? How do you handle this?
49: Do you value diversity in the workplace?
50: How would you handle a situation in which a coworker was not accepting of someone else's diversity?
51: Are you rewarded more from working on a team, or accomplishing a task on your own?

Some of the following titles might also be handy:
1. .NET Interview Questions You'll Most Likely Be Asked
2. 200 Interview Questions You'll Most Likely Be Asked
3. Access VBA Programming Interview Questions You'll Most Likely Be Asked
4. Adobe ColdFusion Interview Questions You'll Most Likely Be Asked
5. Advanced Excel Interview Questions You'll Most Likely Be Asked
6. Advanced JAVA Interview Questions You'll Most Likely Be Asked
7. Advanced SAS Interview Questions You'll Most Likely Be Asked
8. AJAX Interview Questions You'll Most Likely Be Asked
9. Algorithms Interview Questions You'll Most Likely Be Asked
10. Android Development Interview Questions You'll Most Likely Be Asked
11. Ant & Maven Interview Questions You'll Most Likely Be Asked
12. Apache Web Server Interview Questions You'll Most Likely Be Asked
13. Artificial Intelligence Interview Questions You'll Most Likely Be Asked
14. ASP.NET Interview Questions You'll Most Likely Be Asked
15. Automated Software Testing Interview Questions You'll Most Likely Be Asked
16. Base SAS Interview Questions You'll Most Likely Be Asked
17. BEA WebLogic Server Interview Questions You'll Most Likely Be Asked
18. C & C++ Interview Questions You'll Most Likely Be Asked
19. C# Interview Questions You'll Most Likely Be Asked
20. C++ Internals Interview Questions You'll Most Likely Be Asked
21. CCNA Interview Questions You'll Most Likely Be Asked
22. Cloud Computing Interview Questions You'll Most Likely Be Asked
23. Computer Architecture Interview Questions You'll Most Likely Be Asked
24. Computer Networks Interview Questions You'll Most Likely Be Asked
25. Core JAVA Interview Questions You'll Most Likely Be Asked
26. Data Structures & Algorithms Interview Questions You'll Most Likely Be Asked
27. Data WareHousing Interview Questions You'll Most Likely Be Asked
28. EJB 3.0 Interview Questions You'll Most Likely Be Asked
29. Entity Framework Interview Questions You'll Most Likely Be Asked
30. Fedora & RHEL Interview Questions You'll Most Likely Be Asked
31. GNU Development Interview Questions You'll Most Likely Be Asked
32. Hibernate, Spring & Struts Interview Questions You'll Most Likely Be Asked
33. HTML, XHTML and CSS Interview Questions You'll Most Likely Be Asked
34. HTML5 Interview Questions You'll Most Likely Be Asked
35. IBM WebSphere Application Server Interview Questions You'll Most Likely Be Asked
36. iOS SDK Interview Questions You'll Most Likely Be Asked
37. Java / J2EE Design Patterns Interview Questions You'll Most Likely Be Asked
38. Java / J2EE Interview Questions You'll Most Likely Be Asked
39. Java Messaging Service Interview Questions You'll Most Likely Be Asked
40. JavaScript Interview Questions You'll Most Likely Be Asked
41. JavaServer Faces Interview Questions You'll Most Likely Be Asked
42. JDBC Interview Questions You'll Most Likely Be Asked
43. jQuery Interview Questions You'll Most Likely Be Asked
44. JSP-Servlet Interview Questions You'll Most Likely Be Asked
45. JUnit Interview Questions You'll Most Likely Be Asked
46. Linux Commands Interview Questions You'll Most Likely Be Asked
47. Linux Interview Questions You'll Most Likely Be Asked
48. Linux System Administrator Interview Questions You'll Most Likely Be Asked
49. Mac OS X Lion Interview Questions You'll Most Likely Be Asked
50. Mac OS X Snow Leopard Interview Questions You'll Most Likely Be Asked
51. Microsoft Access Interview Questions You'll Most Likely Be Asked

52. Microsoft Excel Interview Questions You'll Most Likely Be Asked
53. Microsoft Powerpoint Interview Questions You'll Most Likely Be Asked
54. Microsoft Word Interview Questions You'll Most Likely Be Asked
55. MySQL Interview Questions You'll Most Likely Be Asked
56. NetSuite Interview Questions You'll Most Likely Be Asked
57. Networking Interview Questions You'll Most Likely Be Asked
58. OOPS Interview Questions You'll Most Likely Be Asked
59. Operating Systems Interview Questions You'll Most Likely Be Asked
60. Oracle DBA Interview Questions You'll Most Likely Be Asked
61. Oracle E-Business Suite Interview Questions You'll Most Likely Be Asked
62. ORACLE PL/SQL Interview Questions You'll Most Likely Be Asked
63. Perl Interview Questions You'll Most Likely Be Asked
64. PHP Interview Questions You'll Most Likely Be Asked
65. PMP Interview Questions You'll Most Likely Be Asked
66. Python Interview Questions You'll Most Likely Be Asked
67. RESTful JAVA Web Services Interview Questions You'll Most Likely Be Asked
68. Ruby Interview Questions You'll Most Likely Be Asked
69. Ruby on Rails Interview Questions You'll Most Likely Be Asked
70. SAP ABAP Interview Questions You'll Most Likely Be Asked
71. Selenium Testing Tools Interview Questions You'll Most Likely Be Asked
72. Silverlight Interview Questions You'll Most Likely Be Asked
73. Software Repositories Interview Questions You'll Most Likely Be Asked
74. Software Testing Interview Questions You'll Most Likely Be Asked
75. SQL Server Interview Questions You'll Most Likely Be Asked
76. Tomcat Interview Questions You'll Most Likely Be Asked
77. UML Interview Questions You'll Most Likely Be Asked
78. Unix Interview Questions You'll Most Likely Be Asked
79. UNIX Shell Programming Interview Questions You'll Most Likely Be Asked
80. VB.NET Interview Questions You'll Most Likely Be Asked
81. XLXP, XSLT, XPATH, XFORMS & XQuery Interview Questions You'll Most Likely Be Asked
82. XML Interview Questions You'll Most Likely Be Asked

For complete list visit
www.vibrantpublishers.com

NOTES